Business Intelligence and Analytics for Law Firms:

Insights for a shifting business ecosystem

EDITED BY FRANCESCA RAMADAN

Commissioning editor
Alex Davies

Editorial assistant
Francesca Ramadan

Published by
Globe Law and Business Ltd
3 Mylor Close
Horsell
Woking
Surrey GU21 4DD
United Kingdom
Tel: +44 20 3745 4770
www.globelawandbusiness.com

ISBN: 978-1-78358-344-7
A catalogue record for this book is available from the British Library

Contents

Contents

Executive summary

We live in an information age. In both our personal and professional lives, we are consistently bombarded with data in various forms; through our interactions with technologies in our homes and workplaces, we are also constantly generating data that will in turn be harvested and displayed to another. Information has arguably become the most valuable resource of all businesses, as technology grows in sophistication and utilization, the world becomes ever more globalized, and economies continue the shift to operating on the acquiring and exchanging of knowledge. With the right data – and the appropriate tools for gathering and processing it – the key to success for any organization seems to be within easy reach. When correctly utilized, data analytics can contribute to the construction of meaningful information patterns, identifying opportunities to boost profitability, and improve product quality and service delivery. However, the essential problem lies in the sheer quantity of available data. With such a tsunami of information, it can be difficult to know where to start. What exactly is the "right" data? Which tools and methodologies can we use to measure it effectively?

For the majority of law firms, these are difficult questions to answer. Cultural norms in the profession and the traditionally risk-averse, occasionally technophobic, nature of many lawyers are both obstacles to the alteration of working practices to encompass data analysis. However, despite the fact that global economies are in recovery and the demand for legal services is picking up, the marketplace remains incredibly tough, and processing of data has become essential for those firms wishing to retain a competitive edge. It is therefore critical for the legal profession as a whole to initiate a cultural change and acquire new skills in order to survive in a dynamic landscape being transformed by technological disruption and economic pressure. *Business Intelligence and Analytics for Law Firms: Insights for a shifting business ecosystem* is the ideal tool to begin the implementation of this development, featuring advice and observations from pioneers in this relatively uncharted territory. Expert guidance is also complemented by examples of best practice – something which is typically difficult to gain access to, considering the frequently sensitive nature of business intelligence processes.

Both practicing lawyers and those who manage law firms and law departments make decisions and judgments with incomplete information. Faced with such uncertainty, is there a way to improve decision-making? Other industries can provide guidance for the legal profession, with artificial intelligence and machine learning methodologies transforming decision-making practices and improving shareholder value. In chapter 1, Aileen Leventon – a practicing lawyer and management consultant – and Gill Eapen – an engineer and economist – show how those who embrace an analytically driven risk, value and resource management process could gain significant competitive advantages in this age of possibilities and in the presence of high uncertainty.

From pitches and proposals, to deepening client relationships through client targeting and cross-selling, data and technology are changing the way firms operate. In conjunction with this, we are also aware that the sheer amount of information available can be a problem in itself – how can we be sure where is the best place to start? In chapter 2, Jennifer Roberts – data scientist at Intapp - lays out ways in which the power of data can be harvested within your firm for strategic client-centric efforts, and explores ways to initiate the change and areas in which technology can help you and your firm excel.

"Business intelligence" differs from "practice intelligence." Running a law firm like a practice often comes at the expense of maintaining a business mindset. Law firms are a profit paradise, but the field is changing; new forces that present new challenges are quickly gaining momentum. Pricing pressure and fierce competition have long been a reality in the business world. In chapter 3, Ariela Tannenbaum – principal at Edge International and CEO of Advanced Financial Analytics – delves into the ways that law firms can develop and take full advantage of the financial intelligence that predominates in the world of big business and succeed in the new normal of the legal practice realm.

The right kind of information can contribute to a firm's success in many different ways. While emotional intelligence may seem an oddity for consideration in the discussion of business analytics for lawyers, well-documented data establishes the importance of these skills in achieving the highest levels of performance. There is also evidence to suggest that a lawyer's tendency to discount and underperform in these areas can lead to disaster, both on a personal and organizational level.

In chapter 4, principal and founder of Law People Management Ronda Muir argues that developing emotional intelligence provides an avenue for improved mental and physical performance, higher personal and organizational profitability, and a better competitive position – all of which is critical at a time where AI robots are nipping at the lawyer's heels.

The implementation of formal business intelligence and data analytics strategies within law firms continues to increase, including data governance and the use of data visualization dashboards. However, in this relatively new field, direction and real-world examples are sometimes difficult to come across, with many firms unwilling to share their experiences. In chapter 5, Melaina Fireman – senior manager of business intelligence and database services at Goodwin Procter – defies this trend, sharing best practice and lessons learned from the formal BI strategy recently implemented at her firm. Those looking for ways to develop and strengthen a data-driven enhanced culture within their own practice will benefit from the insight into Goodwin Procter's collaborative and agile approach to business intelligence.

Due to today's rapidly changing market for legal services, law firms have engaged a myriad of strategies to adapt and compete. One investment many firms are making is in their marketing and business development department. Over the past few years, business development and marketing has become more of a science than an art — largely due to the availability and abundance of data. Litigation and transactional analytics tools allow users to benchmark themselves against their peers, receive alerts about potential new business, and assess litigation and transactions activity by practice area, volume of matters, and significant clients and industries at large. Chapter 6 by Michelle Murray – chief marketing officer at Cahill Gordon & Reindel LLP – explores four ways legal professionals can harness big data to better identify both opportunities and competitive risks.

It is becoming a more accepted fact that law firms have a strong need for data analvytics. Taking this into account, examples of best practice are invaluable tools in this emerging sphere. In chapter 7, Kesney Fotes, data analytics manager at WilmerHale, provides an extensive overview of the journey undertaken in creating a modern data platform at his firm, a member of the AmLaw 100 list. Discussed within this chapter are some of the pressing issues facing those seeking to improve their operations using BI and analytics, including considerations on the question of build or buy and the quantification of business value.

Business intelligence tools have been instrumental in analyzing historical and current data to assist law firms in both business and operational decisions. However, many firms have been making successful decisions without the use of business intelligence tools for years. Some law firm leaders may say they have always relied on "gut instinct", but sometimes the analysis may suggest that this is not always the best measure for decision making. Chapter 8 by Paige Keith, chief financial officer at Hawkins Parnell Thackston & Young LLP, discusses the challenges law firms face when business intelligence guides them in a direction differing from what they have always done or feel like doing. Furthermore, it will examine ways to reconcile seemingly opposing data with the cultural identity of the firm without undermining either one.

In chapter 9, John Alber – futurist for the Institute for Future of Law Practice – discusses the fundamentals of business intelligence in order to highlight the reason of why BI is undertaken and, more importantly, why it is a key to success. He then outlines the process of "Design Thinking", and how it can be used to help firms evolve their business in the right direction – by questioning and defining the most basic operations of a firm. As developments in technology steadily progress, the question of how firms will interact with and utilize high-end technology to augment their intelligence functions is becoming a key subject for debate.

About the authors

John Alber serves as futurist for the Institute for Future of Law Practice. He was also the first futurist for the International Legal Technology Association. He writes, speaks and consults widely, focusing on finding practical ways to reshape the delivery of legal services to suit a future demanding excellence far beyond substantive legal skills. Prior to his current role, John was a transportation industry CEO. Thereafter, he led Bryan Cave LLP to become one of the most innovative firms in the world, serving as its strategic innovation partner for more than 16 years. John is an Emeritus fellow of the College of Law Practice Management and has received a number of awards, both in the legal field and in information technology generally.

Gill Eapen is the founder and CEO of Decision Options, a leader in artificial intelligence applications in business decision-making. He has over 30 years of experience in strategy, finance, machine learning, artificial intelligence, engineering and general management, and has advised clients in a broad range of industries, including aerospace, pharmaceuticals and financial and legal services. Gill is the author of two textbooks, *Decision Options: The Art and Science of Making Decisions* and *Flexibility: Flexible Companies for the Uncertain World*, which address the theory and practice of real options in economic valuation and investment decision-making and the structure, systems, and strategies needed for companies to survive and succeed in an increasingly uncertain world, respectively. His blog "Scientific Sense" is followed by people in over 150 countries, and he is a frequent speaker at conferences worldwide on subjects of strategy, innovation, economics, and analytics.

Melaina Fireman helps organizations make better decisions. As Goodwin Procter's senior manager of business intelligence and database services, she focuses on data management, business intelligence, knowledge management and data governance best practices. She provides technical leadership and serves as a data visualization champion to legal and administrative departments while optimizing data solutions in support of the business strategy. Prior to joining Goodwin in 2003, Melaina has held database management and data warehouse positions in the United States and Europe.

Kesney Fontes is the data analytics manager at WilmerHale. He has over 20 years of experience with enterprise systems, focusing the first part of his career on Document Management Systems (DMS) for large organizations and managing a team of engineers responsible for the implementation and integration of third party applications. His experience ranges from document management, enterprise search, finance and HR, to other legal vertical systems. Most recently, he has created a data warehouse solution, including ETL, reporting and Tabular cubes, leveraging PowerBI. He manages a team of developers maintaining the data analytics infrastructure and partners with business areas such as finance, practice management and legal project management in support of the organization's data solution.

Paige Keith is a business executive with extensive experience leading financial and accounting operations of law firms, including planning, reporting, billing, tax compliance, and accounts payable. Before becoming a chief financial officer at Hawkins Parnell Thackston & Young LLP, she spent 15 years in various management roles responsible for developing and implementing strategic initiatives. She has also overseen client relations and the delivery of legal services, emphasizing the design and integration of consumer-centric business models and technology. Paige studied at Southern Methodist University in Dallas, Texas, where she earned an MBA from the Cox School of Business and a BS in mechanical engineering with biomedical specialization.

Aileen Leventon is a business counselor to the legal industry and a practicing lawyer with over 35 years of experience. She advises lawyers and legal operations professionals on strategies to manage and sustain sound financial performance and continuously improve the efficiency of legal work. Recognizing the impact of artificial intelligence techniques to improve the quality of decision-making, Aileen launched Predictive Legal Economics in 2017. She collaborates with Gill Eapen, the founder of Decision Options, to apply proven techniques from other industries to create value in the legal industry. Now a principal of Edge International, she began her consulting career at PricewaterhouseCoopers LLP after obtaining her MBA. Her work at PwC served as the template for the founding of the General Counsel Roundtable and current approaches to data analytics in the legal profession. As both a project manager, speaker and collaborator, Aileen has actively participated in many pro bono projects for the Bar, CLOC, ACC and the ABA.

Ronda Muir, principal and founder of Law People Management, is one of the country's leading authorities on lawyer personalities and solutions to both traditional and emerging people management challenges that are unique to the legal industry. Muir draws from years of practicing law in New York and Europe, both as outside counsel and in-house counsel, coupled with advanced study in behavioral science. Nationally recognized for her identification of emerging industry trends, she is a frequent speaker, an award-winning author and publishes www.LawPeopleBlog.com, a recognized resource for the legal community. Ronda's best-selling book *Beyond Smart: Lawyering with Emotional Intelligence*, published by the American Bar Association, is the first comprehensive guide to understanding, using and raising emotional intelligence in the context of the practice of law.

Michelle Murray spent 14 years in institutional fixed income sales on a trading desk before changing paths to become the leader of Cahill Gordon & Reindel LLP's marketing, business development and communications department. At Cahill, Michelle works closely with the firm's executive leadership, management and practice groups to develop and execute strategic business and client-focused initiatives that advance the firm's objectives. She directs all aspects of the firm's branding and marketing strategy, client relations, alumni relations, communications and public relations, digital marketing and social media. Michelle is currently the chair-elect of the LMA's New York Local Steering Committee, and is a certified White Belt in Legal Lean Sigma and Project Management.

Jennifer Roberts is a data scientist at Intapp. She is responsible for the analytics and research component that supports thought leadership and new initiatives. Leveraging her skills to advocate, evangelize and build data-fueled products and insight, she examines the legal industry to drive analytical intelligence that informs strategic decisions and solves organizational needs. Prior to joining Intapp, Jennifer was responsible for innovation and development of thought leadership content at

Thomson Reuters. Jennifer received her Master's degree from Humphrey School of Public Policy, with an emphasis on statistical methodology and performance measures within various industries.

Ariela Tannenbaum is the CEO of Advanced Financial Analytics, a consultancy firm focusing on enhancing law firms' profitability, and principal at Edge International. She has over 25 years of top tier leadership experience working with global Fortune 500 companies, instilling the financial intelligence and discipline used by the most successful organizations in the world to drive performance at law firms. Prior to establishing Advanced Financial Analytics, Ariela served as executive vice president of finance at one for the largest companies in the world and global head of finance of its $2 trillion investment management subsidiary for over 14 years.

Chapter 1: Learning from clients to improve decision-making in the legal industry

By Gill Eapen, founder and CEO of Decision Options, and Aileen Leventon, principal at Edge International

Practicing lawyers and those who manage law firms and law departments make decisions and judgments with incomplete information. When clients seek legal advice to guide their business decisions, lawyers frequently respond with: "It depends." Those who manage law firms seek to grow profits by increasing revenue and controlling costs. Those who manage legal operations are charged with implementing tactics to add value in serving the business while also optimizing legal spending, in pursuit of adding to the company's bottom line. The management of a legal organization requires a great many trade-offs in allocating resources, assessing risks and making choices to formulate high impact strategy. Both the practice of law and the stewardship of an organization require assumptions based on incomplete and dynamic information. Both entail the use of appropriate heuristics, data and analytics.

Faced with many choices and much uncertainty, is there a way to improve decision-making? When a lawyer states that "It depends," how might we go beyond intuition, personal experience and cognitive biases to use the right kind of information to foster better outcomes? In law practice there are many possibilities: the lawyer's experience; empirical information; the client's risk profile and tolerance for complexity; and the lawyer's judgment.

Management questions about allocating resources, staffing, lateral hiring, insourcing and outsourcing, business development, and pricing involve similar challenges. Should we benchmark against others, predict the future, or use statistical models from which to draw inferences? Have we framed a valid hypothesis to ask the right questions in using statistical models?

Experience from outside the legal industry

Many believe that the legal industry is different. Lawyers generally and law firm management in particular are excellent at spotting issues, identifying risk, and marshalling the power of precedent. The case for change is evolving slowly, but the legal industry tends to see the solution as a technology choice, when in fact it is about making better business decisions. The legal industry appears to be lagging compared to other industries in the use of rigorous methods from the world of empirical analysis, statistical modelling, econometrics and data-driven decision-making. These are not technology solutions; they are a different way of solving problems in uncertain and evolving situations.

Experience in other industries provides guidance for the legal profession. Artificial intelligence and machine learning methodologies have transformed decision-making practices and improved shareholder value for companies in industries ranging from consulting, healthcare, food manufacturing, biosciences, automotive, and agriculture, to name a few. Combining the latest ideas in machine and deep learning, it is possible to develop predictive models that assist in answering questions that impact legal and business risk and value.

This chapter provides examples from other industries and then suggests ways in which the same methodology may be applied in the legal industry. We start with two basic case studies:

Industry: Professional services consulting

Challenge

Pricing of engagements is inconsistent, often driven by the fear of the managing director failing to be retained by the client, and profitability of engagements fail to meet economic targets for profitability required by the firm.

Question

What's the optimum price for an engagement based on all available characteristics, including but not limited to project and client attributes, availability of internal personnel and skills, and strategic aspects of the relationship with the client?

Solution

Development of a robust pricing model that provides standards to managing directors to improve the profitability of engagements.

Impact

A more disciplined approach to pricing based on predicted optimum price providing decision-guidance for managing directors to take into account any qualitative considerations, with improved profitability of engagements.

Industry: Healthcare

Challenge

Develop a strategy for managing disease risk for patients in such modalities as hypertension, diabetes and COPD. In the current regime of increasing value and quality-based payments, providers are under increasing pressure to enhance patient outcomes while simultaneously optimizing the economics of their practices. It is possible that the industry will slowly migrate to full capitation and providers will be forced to use technology to fundamentally transform their practices.

Question

What is the probability that patient will develop certain conditions in the future and, if this is known systematically, how can providers proactively engage with such patients to prevent diseases or to improve outcomes?

Solution

Artificial intelligence-based agents constantly operating on electronic medical record data can provide decision guidance to physicians to manage the patient populations. Such agents can also get better over time based on newly arriving data and past experiences.

Impact

Physician practices can move into personalized care to manage their patients to improve outcomes patient by patient, enhance overall population health as well as optimize the economics of their practices.

Taking these case studies further, consider more complex business environments:

Food manufacturing

How do companies make decisions that impact a company's compliance with government regulations, resource allocation, corporate reputation, as well as the cost of a product to consumers? Assessments about legal and business risk factor significantly in the management decisions in the food manufacturing industry. The quality of the manufacturing process is critical, and getting it right involves many choices and trade-offs. How many quality assurance professionals are required per number of units produced? Are there factors that impact quality (or defects in manufacturing) based on the season, the work shift, the demographics of personnel? Which regulations pose the biggest risks if there are compliance failures? Can those risks be quantified? Some of these questions have been considered in the application of lean manufacturing practices, but the decision-making process has been improved through a systematic approach based on a predictive economic analysis. Shareholder value is enhanced when a company makes effective trade-offs between productivity and risk to enhance the manufacturing workflow.

Biosciences

Consider an even more complex challenge faced by the biosciences industry, which invests hundreds of billions a year on research and development programs that aim to discover and develop new therapies to prevent, diagnose, cure, or alleviate diseases affecting humans and animals. These expenses are spread over a long time, often decades, from idea generation stage to marketed product. With only one out of over 100 ideas turning into a commercially viable product, the risks are enormous. Traditional financial analytics methods and qualitative methods are insufficient. A focus on building systems that collect large amounts of data to tackle uncertainty is also misguided and has led to significant data intensity, which has not necessarily increased the quality of decisions. The ability to make these decisions more effectively – how to best allocate money, people and time – is a driver of competitive advantage.

To meet the objective, R&D programs target to develop a number of different "candidates" that may fit a general profile. Each candidate has expectations in terms of the end products, delivery mechanisms, pricing, and other factors. Each candidate also has a project plan with various investment options and schedules. Adding further to the complexity, the development plan for each candidate may also include many internal departments and partners outside the company who may provide resources and services specific to the program.

The complexity of these development plans creates significant uncertainty about outcomes – but along with such uncertainty comes considerable opportunity to build managerial flexibility into the design and execution of such programs. Using the Decisions Options® methodology, author Gill Eapen has achieved significant improvements in maximizing the value from limited resources as well as making decision-processes nearly real-time in some of the largest life sciences companies.

Translation to the legal industry

Powerful tools that have had impact on shareholder value in consulting, health care, food manufacturing, biosciences are available to the legal industry as well. We consider below some "use cases" in the management of a law firm and law department, and the substantive practice of law as well.

Pricing matters and portfolios of matters

The experience in the professional services consulting industry is directly relevant to the legal industry. The sources of the data may be different, but both have fragmented incomplete systems as well as qualitative data sources that are capable of analysis. Although the model starts with historical information, once put into service the model updates continuously. By building in to the system the opportunity to learn from ongoing experience, the model adjusts and offers insights to provide real-time guidance.

Case strategy

The example from healthcare provides guidance in developing a case strategy. Most cases settle or there is a payout after trial and appeal. If we treat this as analogous to the outcome in the healthcare example, we have the parallel challenge of assessing whether there is an optimal amount of legal work and associated fees and expenses. Is there a certain point at which further work on a matter will not produce a better outcome? Are there certain cases that should be handled differently because of their attributes?

Artificial intelligence-based agents are able to operate on data from both a client's docket and reported cases (whether they are court documents or announcements in the media) to provide guidance to lawyers about pursuing or settling a case. These AI agents improve over time based on newly-arriving data and past experiences. A client could look at all its cases of a certain type (all products cases; all employment cases) to make decisions about when to settle a case. In the case of contracts with suppliers, the analysis could expand to assess whether there are attributes that indicate potential disputes (e.g. medical conditions) and whether business people involved in the arrangement might be counselled to conduct themselves in a manner that mitigates risk.

Hiring

Just as the results of R&D efforts create the value in the biosciences industry, lawyers are the most valuable asset for a law firm and a law department. Is there a way to predict success beyond the current methods?

There are many choices to be considered in making decisions about who should be hired, at what level (partner or associate), and when. Once a hire is made, what kind of integration efforts does the firm make to support laterals? Are there programs to foster skills development in critical substantive, business generation and other core areas? What impact does such factors as office location, virtual work and demographics have on success? These and other questions are asked every day; but they may all be the wrong questions because they only reflect the biases of the firm's managers.

Decision Options® is an approach that analyzes data from a wide range of systems, such as personnel files, time and billing systems, dockets, new matter intake records, and so many more. From this, it is possible to develop a predictive model that looks for patterns in the data of the organization (i.e., law firm, law department, practice group, office location). After patterns emerge it is possible to formulate hypotheses to test, and ultimately develop a decision-making methodology. The data provides insight that is continuously updated as it is used to gain an unbiased look into the firm; the model self-adjusts over time. This is a machine learning model, which and can add value to the law firm by getting a better return on its investment in its principal asset – its lawyers.

Staffing

What is the best mix of lawyers and other professionals for staffing a matter? Does the type of matter, location, client, existence of a client team or relationship partner, or the amount at stake make a difference? The approach used in the food manufacturing example is relevant because that situation involved trade-offs that affected quality, productivity, risk and economics. The same applies in law practice and matter management.

Staffing decisions are often based on who has the right skills, whether they are available and whether they meet the client's expectations about the profile of a team. Although these qualitative choices are important, do they necessarily create the best outcome in levels of client satisfaction? And if a staffing model is adjusted, what are the trade-offs in quality, risk and profitability and pricing structures?

Conclusion

Clients are harnessing available data to make more effective decisions and improve their financial results. Typically, the data is unstructured, incomplete, and pulled from many different systems within the company. Publicly-available data may also be used to enrich the analysis. The legal industry is well positioned to learn from the experience of its clients.

When there is data – even when there are gaps and the data is "dirty" – there is information to be found. Using well-established tools from mathematics and combining it with extraordinary increases in computing power, the profiled companies are better positioned to achieve and maintain a competitive advantage. The legal industry should take advantage of the invaluable opportunities that have enabled improved outcomes and economic results for their clients. The lawyers who take advantage of these techniques will be better positioned to achieve a sustainable competitive advantage and add value to the clients they serve.

Chapter 2:
Achieving client-centricity through data and technology

By Jennifer Roberts, data scientist at Intapp

Client-centricity isn't a new idea in legal. Clients have always been the center of a law firm. However, in recent years, as clients have gained the reins and the market has become increasingly more competitive, the underpinning principles of what it means to be client-centric are separating the good from the great. As a strategic approach, client-centricity focuses on creating a superior experience for the client, placing the client as the center of the firm's philosophy, operations, and ideas. Bringing these elements together empowers firms to properly articulate their value and meet the more sophisticated client demands. This is made increasingly more important as firms report that their single best source of business is additional work from existing clients; it is not just about landing new work, but rather about nurturing the relationship. After all, keeping a client isn't just about loyalty these days.

In all other industries, serving, retaining, and winning new business happens through a combination of a strong value proposition, customer experience, and product excellence. This does not waver in the case of law firms – the product is the lawyer or, on a more granular level, the billable hour and how that transpires into the firm's collective experience and expertise delivered by the lawyer. It is no surprise that data is leading the charge in these endeavors as organizations strive to paint a complete picture of the client and develop a service model to engage with them.

Learning from outside the industry, all signs point to data but not executed in a vacuum; the people and process around the consumption of data act as a buttress for success. In a recent 2018 Law Firm Growth Enablement research in collaboration with Intapp and Calibrate Legal, 80 marketing and business development executives were asked how data is currently being used. As seen below, a majority use the data for one-to-many efforts that, while beneficial, are not perceived as client-centric in nature because these lower value efforts are not tailored to specific needs of the client.

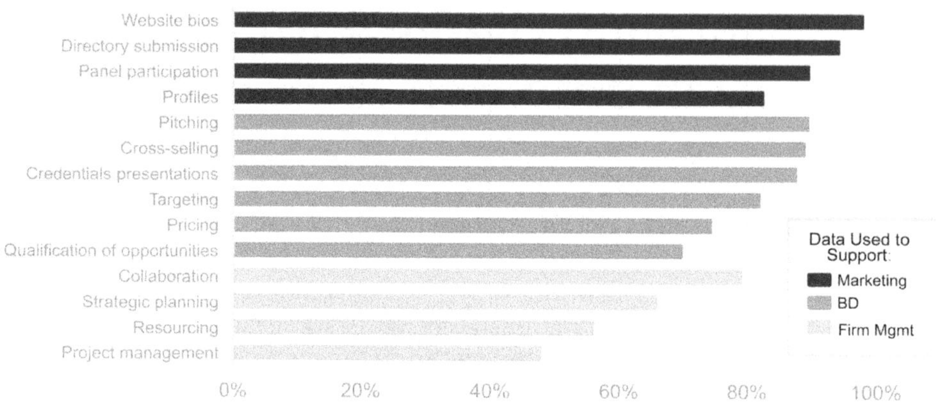

Figure 1: What is this data currently used for?

When asked how firms intend to use the data in the future, collaboration, strategic planning, resourcing, and project management all rose to the top of the list (nearly the inverse of the chart above!). The importance of these strategic efforts is not lost on marketing and business development. However, barriers continue to get in the way of firms fully realizing the potential.

High-performing firms recognize the potential in reorienting around the client and the firm's collective expertise according to the 2017 Intapp Experience Management survey. The results showed that firms with strong revenue growth are leveraging systems, processes, and data to systematically innovate the way the firm delivers on client demands. Moreover, firms that are pulling away from the pack on traditional metrics (revenue, realization, demand) are also spending more on marketing and business development as well as technology.[1]

These investments are coming in the form of AI, data, analytics, and all the other strategic initiatives from above where firms recognize data can help drive. So how does a firm unlock the power of data and truly harness the disruptive potential?

It all begins with data...

First, the data must be identified; in order to do this, firms must understand the clients' journey – an exercise that is key to discovering where a firm can extract insight (i.e. data) and interject value (i.e. key account programs, ROI). For example, a keen understanding of how the client interfaces with the firm and even the subtle differences among practice groups and relationship partners can provide impactful data on levers to engage on certain subsections of clients; in turn you understand the type of services target groups respond best to and what to change if certain clients are at risk. This analysis can also help drive efficiency plays, as it uncovers where there might be overlaps in data capture efforts (think about the information captured at Intake and then again that the library and BD enter on client demographics).

It also requires taking an inventory of all the systems where data currently flows through the firm, including: document management systems, time and billing systems, business acceptance, time entry, active directory, etc. Beyond these systems, ad hoc data exercises happening at the firm should be taken into account as well. This brings to mind client feedback programs – over 60 percent of firms have client feedback programs and the remaining all plan to implement in some fashion over the next 12 months.[2] Most of the efforts are manual, primarily interviews by third parties and in-house (BD and/or leadership). Despite the efforts underway, a majority of firms are only using the data for at-risk accounts. A large proportion (nearly 25 percent) report not using the data at all. Firms are missing out on a wealth of knowledge that can enhance insights at the firm. Think about what an in-depth understanding of a client can provide to the firm by means of sentiment and engagement. Adding additional attributes through third-party data only further enhances the overall dataset. Data aggregated by the likes of D&B and other providers offer industry codes, company size, revenue, and other publicly reported records that provides additive information to help draw segments around a firm's client portfolio. Overlaying the inventory of systems with a map of the clients' journey provides a holistic understanding of what makes up subsets of clients and the way they are served – where are weaknesses (declining realization? Slowing work over time? Displeasure with a recent engagement?) and where are opportunities (what do we know about what happy clients look like? How do we replicate?).

Once the data is identified, answers to these questions can quickly bubble to the surface. In the beginning, most efforts are small-scale and depend on the skillsets available; however, they can still have massive impact. For example, it is known commonly in the industry that 80 percent of a firm's revenue comes from 20 percent of the firm's clients, so spending time to understand this 20 percent can provide valuable insights into what revenue-driving clients look like in terms of demographics and behaviors, as well as type of work profile. These insights help to understand the services provided so that strategic efforts can be designed to target groups as well as become systematic in outreach when you've found a model that works (it is worth noting that models can vary by practice and industry, since the clients served differ).

Although static, descriptive statistics on various subsets of data – be it the 20 percent and/or a cross-section of attributes – can begin to define segments and the associated behaviors and buying patterns. This can be done by looking at the averages for these subsets across age of relationship, number of practices engaged, lawyers engaged, dominate practices at play – just to name a few low-hanging fruit. Additionally, looking at correlation between practices and lawyers along with propensity to buy various bundles of services (i.e. what mixes of practices are engaged for these types of clients) set the foundation for data-driven cross-selling efforts centered on the client's needs.

These client-centric data exercises can also teach you about firm-wide heuristics that surface in the data that can then be applied as rules when parsing the data. To name a few:

- Industry-wide best practices:
  - 80/20 rule – the aforementioned 80 percent of your revenue comes from 20 percent of your clients; and
  - Rule of 3 – clients who have three or more practices engaged are more likely to bring on new work.
- Firm best practices:
  - Practice combos – certain practices are typically bundled together whereas others act in opposite directions; and
  - Realization – per engagement relative to the portfolio of clients.

Client scoring is another key element in client-centricity as it provides a quick snapshot on the relationship between firm (not just the lawyer) and client. When scoring a client's best practices, suggest bringing in a balance of attributes ranging from financial performance to sentiment. Proxy variables (a variable that serves in place of an unobservable variable) may be necessary in the circumstance that the data isn't available. Examples of proxy variables include realization as a substitution for client's sentiment towards the firm. Specifically, a client with declining realization struggles to justify cost-to-value. Commonly, general counsel speak on panels regarding their relationships with firms and echo the idea that satisfied clients are willing to pay for valuable services. This suggests that strong realization across a client's matters equates to satisfaction with the value of service being provided; the inverse – weak or declining realization –therefore suggests dissatisfaction in the realm of value and acts as an indicator of risk. Bringing together proxy variables to capture some of the less tangible qualitative data alongside financial performance can work together to create a quantitative score that illustrates the strength of the relationship among firm and client.

More sophisticated efforts can digest all this data and deploy higher value analytics – pulling in the attributes and scores already discussed (and beyond) to create predictive models that can be used to suggest cross-selling opportunities, pair pricing to proposals, suggest areas of collaboration, and even identify the right talent for the type of work. These types of initiatives are prevalent in other industries but ahead of the curve in legal, as firms work through barriers that prohibit the space for these types of initiatives.

These examples can be taken in small bites, but when brought together provide depth and breadth around the client helping firms target, define best practices, anticipate needs, and cross-sell with an extreme focus on articulating value to the client.

Leveraging technology

One key component that has not been discussed thus far is technology. Although not explicitly stated, smart technology to bring data together with a basic form of visualization is table stakes to achieve most of what has been discussed. The innovative firms making investments in technology advocate the need to leverage technology to double down. So what type of heavy lifting can technology provide?

Data

AI driven initiatives can help firms normalize data by identifying data weaknesses and applying proxy variables to patch holes. Additionally, these efforts can enhance the robustness of data through AI platforms that leverage machine learning to help code past, present, and future data. Specifically, firms are taking trained data sets from subsets of clean data (say for a practice and/or industry) that has phase and task codes, taxonomies or other areas of service the firm tracks already identified, and using it as a training set to apply these attributes to data that is not coded. Other normalizing efforts can be done to truncate data for better comparisons as well as natural language processes to amplify the data you have and bring narratives to life.

Analytics

Predictive analytics mentioned above require tools designed to carry out higher level statistics. These tools also offer the ability to do cluster analysis, data mining, multivariate regression, forecasting, and machine learning. All in all, these mechanisms afford the firm the ability to pursue predictive and prescriptive analytics providing action through answering "what is next" and "what can be done".

Process improvement

Yet another area to leverage technology is with the process around client-centric efforts. Automation can help bear the burden of more traditional activities that aren't new to business development, such as pitch generation and league table submission. Solutions with sophisticated search capabilities allow firms to search and quickly pull credentials together for their day-to-day needs. With the data necessary to gain a deep understanding of the client, marketing and business development can pull together offerings drawing on the firm's strengths and the clients' desires. Marketing activities like this take up a large portion of time and are often reactive. These efforts can now take on new forms made smarter and easier with technology that leverages intelligent data capture, integration, and workflows to streamline processes.

Process automation can aid in client feedback efforts as well – what is more quintessential to a client-centric approach than the voice of the client? Automation offers the ability to kick off a survey to the lawyer and client upon matter initiation (or perhaps 90 days since last billing) or even along the matter journey to check in, so client and lawyer can remain aligned on expectations.

Systematically capturing client feedback to understand satisfaction is a perfect example of more strategic efforts firms can pursue when they let technology automate various processes. Once the day-to-day fire drills are taken off the table, marketing and business development will have the bandwidth to pursue data-driven exercises that help the firm grow. It is a big step in the client-centric direction as it puts pertinent data to support the client at the firm's fingertips to quickly act and articulate value.

Investing in people

Supporting these efforts elicits cultural changes in the orientation in which firms handle client relationships. With technology facilitating the day-to-day and providing rich intelligence, firms need dedicated resources to support it. In this vein, a growing number of firms are dedicating resources to business development (outside of marketing)[3] and charging them with growing business as the top priority.

As firms become more progressive in their approach to business development, they are also expanding their horizons – specifically bringing pricing and client experience (think net promoter score and client satisfaction) into the business development fold. Looking outside of the industry, it is the natural progression of a client-centric strategy. The outliers, the firms truly innovating in this space, are beginning to provide a packaged offering from pitch and proposal to pricing the work and monitoring the engagement to align value and ensure client satisfaction.

Conclusion

The status quo is no longer enough to land and expand. Firms are being stretched to properly articulate cost-to-value and deliver consistent high-quality offerings. If not reason enough to begin to look inward and become client-centric, many firms report top clients frequently grow revenue at a higher rate than the firm's average, furthering the importance of investing in data to uncover who and what makes up this group. Reaching nirvana involves letting data drive but requires process and people to support and provide a superb service centered on the client's needs – insight gained from a deep understanding of the firm's client segments. This helps across all facets as firms strategically engage with clients to strengthen and grow relationships. Innovative client-centric pursuits are giving those firms willing to make the investment a leg up amongst competition – a smart move at a time when the client is more empowered than ever.

References

1. 2018 Georgetown Report
2. Intapp + Calibrate Legal 2018 Emerging Growth Study
3. 2018 Thomson Reuters Marketing Partner Annual Survey

Chapter 3: Client journey mapping and the customer experience

By Ariela Tannenbaum, CEO of Advanced Financial Analytics and principal at Edge International

Most law firms leave money on the table

Law firms, whether by sheer inexperience or willful ignorance, often either miss opportunities to make money or fail to take advantage of money already earned. And understanding *how much* money they forego in the process? Forget about it.

Let me offer a challenge to all managing partners. Ask yourself the following questions and answer them *out loud to yourself*: do my top clients generate profits for the firm? Do they cover their allocated overhead? How much does each practice area contribute to the partners' profit pool? How much money are we, as a firm, giving up in "write downs" every year? How much does each equity partner give away in "discounts"? And the most sensitive question of all: how much does each partner contribute to the profit pool? While this last question may be unsettling, it is one that managing partners need to explore. For your firm's sake, become comfortable with addressing the uncomfortable.

If you cannot answer these fundamental questions, you are not alone. Lawyers who make a good living do not often feel the need to address latent – or even patent – discrepancies in their business operation. However, it's important to understand that the concepts of the "practice of law" and "running a business" are not at all one and the same.

The legal field now faces a new normal, with unfamiliar dynamics that should prompt managing partners to rise to the occasion and learn some new tricks of the business trade. New challenges that are gaining momentum in the legal field include:

- Increasing price competition and decreasing realization rates;
- Increasing alternative fee arrangements;

- Increasing alternative legal service providers;
- Increasing number of corporate legal departments keeping work in-house; and
- Increasing lateral movements, part-time and contract lawyers.

With BigLaw shutdowns making headlines within the last ten years, even the most conservative law firms are realizing that they must take on a strategic business approach just to survive – much less thrive – in the face of the new normal.

Many firms advance their tech "bells and whistles" to do the trick, while others outsource marketing efforts and turn to professional consultants. Some firms hire COOs. While law firms are starting to welcome business world influence in enhanced technology and marketing functions, they should consider the power of business intelligence that business CEOs use religiously to make decisions with conviction.

Over the past few months, I met with managing partners of several law firms and shared some tricks of the trade, including a financial overview similar to the one used regularly in the business world and which I tailored to the dynamics and specific needs of law firms. The partners offered the following feedback:

- "The heavens just opened."
- "This is fascinating."
- "We have been blind!"
- "Wow!"
- "This is gold."

While I would love to believe that I have the capacity to open the heavens, there were no magic beans involved. Rather, I presented the power of financial intelligence as an invaluable decision-making tool. It captivates those who have never engaged it.

My 25 years of experience in a financial leadership role, mainly and most recently as the global head of finance of a multi-trillion-dollar investment firm, have enabled me to develop and test the effectiveness of a variety of financial models and disciplines to enhance the bottom line.

Become a "Fortune 500" law firm

For a firm to earn an AMLaw 200 rank, it could hire many attorneys and increase revenue; however, such a distinction does not equate to profitability. Some named firms have profit margins of 20 percent – not exactly backflip-worthy. Fortune 500 companies, on the other hand, focus on profitability growth and strong margins.

But how can law firms increase profitability? Mandating an increased billable hour requirement is a short-sighted non-answer. Instead, managing partners can examine their firms through a forward-thinking financial lens. Fortune 500 companies are not in a profit paradise, or at least they do not behave as though they are. To the contrary, Fortune 500 companies are in a constant state of doubt and incessant inquiry: how are we doing today? How are we doing now versus last quarter? What about now versus last year? How is the competition doing? Are our prices optimal? Where are we heading in both the short- and long-term? Those are just a sampling of issues that keep CEOs up at night. The answers to these questions will guide them along a successful path.

Take a look at how your C-level counterparts in the corporate realm gain the essential financial intelligence to maximize profit potential. They use sophisticated financial tools to guide them, to identify their strengths and weaknesses, to define their financial goals, and help them steer their respective firm toward attaining their financial objectives. Your law firm business should operate no differently.

Financial intelligence is your best business decision-making tool

All Fortune 500 companies employ financial analysts, without exception. The finance team works alongside the accounting department. At most companies, financial analysis is a stand-alone department. While most law firms do not need to have a full in-house financial analysis department, law firms do need an internal or external resource in an experienced, self-driven, financial analysis professional – a powerhouse who can develop sophisticated financial models to chart their operation. The same models that work so well for the large successful companies can be scaled and applied to law firms of any size.

Figure 1: Financial management function led by accountants

Identify the cash-cow

To most, the term "cash-cow" simply refers to the one client/practice/lawyer/office that brings in the revenue.

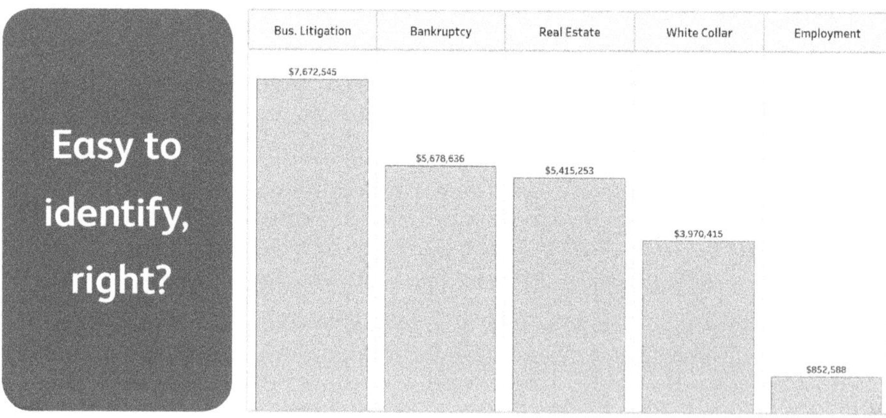

Figure 2: Annual revenue

This is a misleading approach. Not all revenue is "good" revenue. A law firm should be a revenue snob and emphatically *not* chase all revenues. Instead, firms should focus on profitable clients with growth potential. In addition, develop pricing models to *optimize* alternative fee arrangements. Managing partners should know their firms' floor price to increase the "quality" of the revenue.

Law firms must keep a keen eye on profitability and profit margin of all business drivers, and identify trends to appropriately adjust resource allocation.

It is essential to identify and quantify direct cost and consider allocating all overhead expenses across all offices and practices. Partners might be surprised to learn that their firm is potentially subsidizing some practices, offices, or particular partners.

To truly run your law firm as a profit-maximizing business, you must have a pragmatic but holistic overview of firm operations. In certain instances, and for strategic reasons, a law firm may want to keep less profitable business, but "quantifying" cost could be helpful in increasing efficiencies and minimizing the "subsidy." It's only when the firm examines profitability that it can truly identify its "cash-cow".

Figure 3 shows side-by-side revenue (light grey bars) and profits (dark grey bars) of some practices over the course of two years. A sampling of observations that can drive beneficial changes in firm operations:

1. **Business litigation** – revenue increases but profits are flat. A warning sign of declining profit margin;
2. **Bankruptcy** – revenue is lower than business litigation but profits are higher;
3. **White collar defense** – revenue increases but profits decline. A strong indication of diminishing profit margin;
4. **Employment** – running a loss.

Adopting a discipline of periodic examination of the firm's operation is a proven pre-emptive approach to keep all business drivers on course – no surprises, no slippage.

It is imperative that law firm management be well-versed of all relevant performance indicators to facilitate proactive, prompt and decisive action to stay on course, and meet financial objectives.

A disciplined monthly or quarterly review should include at least the following discussion:

- Year-to-date actual P&L results and projections;

- Profitability trends by all drivers: attorneys, practice areas, industries, top clients, and offices;
- Expense analysis;
- Profitability by significant matters;
- Revenue "write-off" analysis: hours worked at billable rate vs hour billed at realized rate; and
- Productivity analysis and trends.

"What if we don't change at all ...
and something magical just happens?"

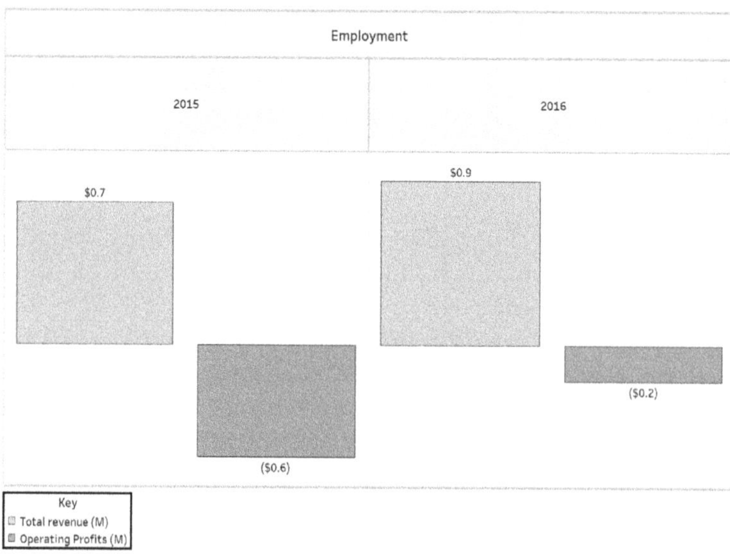

Figure 3: Revenues and profits over two years

Only with these tools can a firm clearly identify its strengths and weaknesses, properly allocate resources and investments, increase revenue and efficiencies, and maximize profit.

In his article "How Firms Should Be Measuring the Profitability of Matters" in *The American Lawyer* (July 28, 2017), strategist Hugh Simons examines how firms typically track matter profitability and opines that firms should focus on margin per partner hour. I agree. His proposed method is accurate and drives action.

The erosion of the billable hour or "the dings"

All law firms determine and dictate the parameters of revenue: annual target for billable hours and corresponding billing rate. Projected revenue calculation is simple: the product of billable hours and fee rate less all the "dings".

- First "ding" – the number of recorded client hours is lower than target hours;
- Second "ding" – recorded hours are "shaved" by the partners before they make it to the client; and
- Third "ding" – the billing rate "shrinks" to the realized rate.

These "dings" have a financial value that often trickles down to the bottom line.

How much revenue are you "giving away"? What is the impact of these "dings"? And what is the year-over-year trend of these inefficiencies? The table in Figure 4 overleaf is an illustration of the impact of the firmwide "dings" or revenue adjustments. Reviewing this simple analysis on a regular basis is likely to increase the efficiency of operations significantly and have a direct impact on the bottom line.

Be mindful that the analysis above is just the beginning. The most important step is peeling the onion further to find the core source of the adjustments: the who, where, and why.

A valuable financial analysis will not only evaluate the current year but also highlight the trends to help determine whether the firm is heading in the right direction. Is it building strength or weakness?

Take a look at the chart in Figure 5. At year-end all lawyers are happy: number of hours worked, number of billing hours, billable revenue, and even realized revenue all have increased over prior year.

	Hours	Rate/hr	Total revenue
Target client hours	92,500	$379	$35,016,553
Client hours recorded	90,650	$379	$34,316,222
Recorded hours lower than target hours---->revenue lower by			$ (700,331)
Hours billed	79,429	$379	$30,068,364
Billed hours lower than recorded hours---->revenue lower by			$ (4,247,858)
Hours billed at realized rate	**79,429**	**$342**	**$27,132,855**
Realized rate lower than billed rate ---->revenue lower by			$ (2,935,509)
Magnitude of revenue adjustments			$ (7,883,698)
Impact of revenue adjustments on average profit per partner			**$ (788,370)**

Figure 4: 2017 revenue adjustments

	2015	2016	Y/Y Change
Total number of client hrs. required	92,500	92,500	-
Total number of client hrs. recorded	90,020	90,650	630
Hours recorded vs. required	**97%**	**98%**	
Total number of client hrs. billed	79,142	79,429	287
Y/Y growth			0.4%
Hours billed vs. hours recorded	**88%**	**88%**	
Total Revenue billed	27,137,236	30,068,364	2,931,128
Y/Y growth			11%
Total realized revenue	26,400,364	27,132,855	732,491
Revenue realized vs. billed	97%	90%	
Revenue erosion due to write-downs of hours and fees:			
Variance due to reduced hours: billed vs. required	$ (4,580,244)	$ (4,948,189)	$ (367,945)
Variance due to reduced rate: realized vs. billed	$ (736,872)	$ (2,935,509)	$ (2,198,638)
Total magnitude of revenue adjustments	**$ (5,317,116)**	**$ (7,883,698)**	**$ (2,566,583)**

Figure 5: Annual trend of revenue erosion

However, a closer look at the picture indicates that despite all the great news, beneath the surface, the firm's revenue is eroding. In fact, year after year the magnitude of "write downs" increases and the firm is leaving more money on the table. In 2016 alone, there would be $7.9 million in adjustments – $2.5 million more than in the previous year.

The takeaway? Embrace the discomfort!

Measure your operation to improve the results (Figure 6):

Figure 6: Measuring to improve

Often the evaluation of a law firm's financial health results in both professional and personal discomfort. However, the benefit and power gained more than outweighs this temporary state. Making business decisions based on solid analysis is a strategy that both business and law firm leaders alike need to consider.

The value of profitability extends beyond a paycheck. It is the future health and success of the firm. Solid ratios such as profit per partner, high profit margin, and high profit per attorney make a law firm an attractive place for the better talent that will fuel and maintain future success.

Chapter 4:
Emotional data in the practice of law

By Ronda Muir, principal and founder of Law People Management LLC

You may be wondering what emotional data has to do with the business analytics of lawyering. Business analytics uses data to improve hiring and staffing, make better-informed business decisions, provide superior client service and avoid risk. Those are also the impacts of raising emotional intelligence skills, particularly the recognition of emotional data, which is discussed here.

What is emotional intelligence? Emotional intelligence (EI, also known as emotional quotient or EQ) is the ability to recognize, understand and manage emotions – our own and others' – in order to successfully accomplish goals.

Lawyers are lousy at recognizing emotional data

Let's start with a single datapoint: lawyers are lousy at recognizing emotional data. Of over 500,000 people tested globally, two-thirds were unaware of the emotions they were experiencing at a given time,[1] yet lawyers are significantly worse. On average, it is our lowest emotional intelligence skill.[2] Lawyers' tendency to not only ignore but also suppress their emotions compounds this deficit.[3] Since all other EI skills rely on first identifying accurately the emotions at play, the failure to recognize emotional data undercuts any other EI skills we have or try to develop.

The emotional data we don't recognize includes our and others' physical, mental and behavioral cues that indicate what's afoot emotionally. Physiologically, emotion neurochemicals permeate our bodies within seconds of a triggering event, whether we recognize it or not, making us "vibrate like a tuning fork".[4] Those neurochemicals impact the functioning of our bodies and our minds, including our perceptions[5] and judgment.[5] The triggers of those emotional responses and the response patterns that follow are developed over a lifetime – starting in utero[7] – and are stored in our emotional brain, which processes emotions hundreds of times faster than we can think.[8] Having access to the information in that part of our psyche girds us with important data.

Why is emotional data so useful in the practice of law? We're lawyers, not shrinks or talk show hosts, you might say. As long as our left brains make us methodical and logical (a thoroughly unsubstantiated view, by the way),[9] who cares?

Emotional data is the bedrock for practicing "smart." Relying solely on cognitive cues and skills without the benefit of emotional data subverts a lawyer's potential intelligence. Emotional data is critical to fully understanding the complexities of a situation, such as a job interview, a negotiation, a partner's complaint, a client's dilemma, a judge's query or a witness's testimony. By being "exquisitely sensitive to the impact they are having on others,"[10] leaders can also gain needed information about what those they are leading need and whether their strategies to influence them are working or not.

In a lengthy multistep assessment study of lawyers, judges, law students and clients conducted over six years, University of Southern California – Berkeley law professor Marjorie Shultz and psychology professor Sheldon Zedeck found that most American lawyers are "unlikely to exhibit [the] strong emotional development" that the researchers found necessary to practice law well.[11] Their conclusion was that the many important personal and relationship emotional management skills needed to practice law successfully far outweigh those few cognitive attributes that lawyers generally have and that law schools recognize and develop. And those critical skills rely on starting with accurate emotional data.

It is simply not enough to be cognitively smart. Daniel Goleman, an early advocate for emotional intelligence, acknowledges the role of IQ in many professions but reiterates the value that EI adds: "It typically takes an IQ about 115 or above to be able to handle the cognitive complexity facing an accountant, a physician or a top executive. But here's the paradox: once you're in a high-IQ position, intellect loses its power to determine who will emerge as a productive employee or an effective leader. For that, how you handle yourself and your relationships – in other words, the emotional intelligence skill set – matters more than your IQ. In a high-IQ job pool, soft skills… mark those who emerge as outstanding."[12]

As consultant Dr Larry Richard has written: "Being an intellectually smart lawyer is the mere table stakes to get into the game of BigLaw. To succeed on a sustained basis, today's lawyer needs to develop EI skills."[13]

Since emotional cues are usually available to us sooner than our rational thoughts, the ability to recognize them also provides a timeliness advantage – helping us reach an informed conclusion more quickly. A famous study called the Iowa Gambling Task, conducted by the world-renowned neuroscientist Antonio Damásio, illustrates that advantage. Participants were presented with four virtual decks of cards. With each card, they would either win or lose money, the goal being to win the most in the shortest time. The decks differed in their rates of wins and losses. Most participants could verbally identify the winning decks after fifty selections. However, measurements of galvanic skin responses showed that after only ten selections, long before they were cognitively aware whether decks were winners or losers, participants registered a physical "stress" reaction when approaching the losing decks. In other words, their emotions were accurately signaling the losing decks well before their cognitive brains could, giving participants who were attuned to their own emotional cues a significant head start.[14]

Emotional data paves the way for superior client service and higher profitability

The legions of firings and complaints because of lawyers' "personalities," unresponsiveness and communication failures testify to the emotional neglect many lawyers exhibit toward their clients. Emotionally intelligent lawyers have the opportunity to outpace their competition just by using emotional intelligence skills that are not widely evident in the profession.

As David Maister – the professional services guru – has said, hiring a lawyer is an "emotional act".[15] That is, getting a client and maintaining a loyal client relationship requires a lawyer to emotionally engage. Emotionally engaging with a client requires that lawyers are attuned to their own and the client's emotional cues. Lawyers who can register the emotional turbulence clients face, who can commiserate, explain sympathetically the issues and options, and help guide the client through daunting legal moves will establish a bond that clients will find valuable and that the efficiencies of technology cannot offer.

It is the growth of technology-assisted lawyering, in fact, that will drive increasing demand – both from outside and in-house clients – for lawyers with emotionally intelligent relationship skills. As a *Harvard Business Review* article proclaims: "The Rise of AI Makes Emotional Intelligence More Important".[16]

Gaining that single skill of accurately reading emotional cues can start a lawyer down the path of better client service and its attendant financial rewards. Essentially, lawyers with those skills can charge handsomely for such a bespoke service. Study after study confirms that both individuals and organizations with higher EI are more likely to be profitable.[17] Baker McKenzie pursued an emotional intelligence professional development program for its lawyers after the recession that raised its revenues to all-time highs and that it continues to benefit from.[18] More recently, Harvard Law Professor Heidi Gardner followed a global law firm to confirm statistically that those lawyers with the EI skills to successfully collaborate were the ones who had the highest revenues, and their firms also realized greater profitability.[19]

Having emotional intelligence can't compensate for engaging in willful misconduct, but lawyers who are able to recognize emotional cues can raise their ethical behavior and lower their liability risk as well, both of which improve bottom line results.[20] Research shows that the emotionally intelligent act more ethically[21] in that they more accurately see and assess the risks involved,[22] recognize when and how others are making ethical decisions,[23] and recognize and deal better with the emotional fallout from their own choices, especially when they are ignoring or acting against personal values,[24] which lawyers may do in advocating for clients.

New, expansive ABA professional conduct rules regarding harassment and discrimination in connection with legal practices[25] amount to a waiting ambush of massive proportions in settings where emotional cues are unseen or ignored. We never get to the question of whether he/she indicated "no" but actually meant "yes" if we start with the proposition that our poor lawyer wouldn't be able to read either. S/he is just blindly acting out impulses without the benefit of recognizing feedback.

Most importantly, emotionally intelligent lawyers can learn to communicate better, as doctors have,[26] avoiding the number one reason for disciplinary actions and malpractice claims in the US and Canada.[27]

Lawyers suffer the highest distress levels

Here's another datapoint: lawyers officially suffer the highest documented distress levels of any profession, even substantially above those beleaguered special needs teachers and maligned dentists.

Lawyer distress can undo good client service and personal or firm profitability. Being aware of our own emotional cues is critical to recognizing and moderating our personal distress. Unfortunately, many lawyers miss that information because of their emotional deafness, and the results are widely incapacitating.

The most recent and comprehensive study on lawyer distress,

conducted in 2016 and funded by the Hazelden Betty Ford Foundation and the ABA's Commission on Lawyer Assistance Programs, found that lawyers suffer substantial rates of behavioral health problems. Among 12,825 licensed, employed attorneys, 36.4 percent screened positive at the time for "hazardous, harmful, and potentially alcohol-dependent drinking," a rate substantially higher than among the general population and among physicians and surgeons. Levels of depression at 28 percent, anxiety at 19 percent, and stress at 23 percent at the time were also significantly higher (in some cases, six times) than the general population, and markedly increased from older reports. The most common mental health conditions attorneys reported having experienced over the course of their careers were anxiety (61.1 percent), followed by depression (45.7 percent), social anxiety (16.1 percent), attention deficit hyperactivity disorder (12.5 percent), panic disorder (8 percent), and bipolar disorder (2.4 percent). The report concluded that "the consequences of attorney impairment ... [are] profound and far-reaching." [28]

A National Institute for Occupational Safety and Health study found that male lawyers in the United States are two times more likely to commit suicide than men in the general population.[29]

According to attorney and clinician Patrick R. Krill, Hazelden's architect of the project: "Any way you look at it, this data is very alarming, and paints the picture of an unsustainable professional culture that's harming too many people. Attorney impairment poses risks to the struggling individuals themselves and to our communities, government, economy and society."[30]

The concern starts in law school. A 2014 survey of Yale Law School students found that 70 percent of respondents struggled with mental health issues during their time at law school, and 50 percent indicated that mental health challenges affected their ability to perform academically.[31] Researchers in Australia also found that "Australian law students have higher rates of psychological distress and depression than community members of similar age and sex and that the deterioration in mental health may begin in the first year of study." And they specifically identify lack of EI skills as a determining factor in higher rates of distress.[32]

These distress stats likely are driven by an inability to recognize and deal with the emotional stress of practicing law. Physical impacts of stress include a pounding heartbeat, sweating, rapid breathing, fatigue, restlessness, tension, aching muscles and headaches.[33] The behavioral manifestations include irritability, obsessive thoughts, feelings of inadequacy, difficulty concentrating, a sense of worry and impending danger, and sleep deprivation. Some attorneys withdraw from peers, friends, and family or engage in maladaptive coping behaviors, such as self-medicating with alcohol and other substances. Living with this level of tension is correlated with heart disease and other illnesses and has also been demonstrated to shorten our lives.[34]

These levels of stress also clearly interfere with even minimal performance levels.[35] One neuropsychologist compares chronic stress to "fine sand being drizzled into the brain... it'll freeze up at some point."[36] Math and language abilities drop as much as 50 percent; memories, both short- and long-term suffer; decision-making becomes compromised.[37]

Would you like to be the client who entrusts their make-or-break matter to one of these highly distressed lawyers so common in our industry? Would you like to be one of those lawyers' colleagues?

Raising emotional intelligence is a key strategy to significantly improving stress management. That link was established in 1908 and has been consistently confirmed since.[38] Important research published in 2013 found that, as with doctors, lawyers gain significant protection against burnout and job dissatisfaction with higher EI.[39] Those who can recognize their emotional cues can learn to lower their stress levels and are at less risk of suffering from depression.[40] That pays off in greater cognitive functioning, lower blood pressure and better immunity.[41]

As the authors of *The Illicit Relationship of Lawyers and Emotions* concluded: "We are not suffering, as a profession, from our inability to think clearly or analyze properly, we are suffering because we have been trained to ignore our emotional dimension."[42]

In summary, having access to emotional data would put individual lawyers, legal workplaces and the entire industry on better footing for reaching our goals of improving hiring and staffing, making better-informed business decisions, providing superior client service and avoiding risk.

References

1. Bradberry, Travis, and Jean Greaves. *Emotional Intelligence 2.0.*, 26 San Diego, CA: TalentSmart, 2009.
2. Larry Richard, "Herding Cats," Altman Weil Report to Legal Management, 1–12.
3. Sandi Mann, "Emotion at Work: To What Extent Are We Expressing, Suppressing, or Faking It?", *European Journal of Work and Organizational Psychology* 8(3), pp347–369; Debora Cutuli, "Cognitive Reappraisal and Expressive Suppression Strategies Role in Emotion Regulation: An Overview on Their Modulatory Effects and Neural Correlates", *Frontiers in Systems Neuroscience*, 175 (2014), pp59–63.
4. Dr. Candace Pert, *Molecules Of Emotion*, 1997 Touchstone, NY, NY

5. "Emotion and Perception: The Role of Affective Information," Jonathan R. Zadra and Gerald L. Clore, Wiley, *Interdisciplinary Review of Cognitive Sciences.* 2011 Nov-Dec; 2(6): 676–685. Emotions significantly impact perceptions of sound, distance, steepness and other sense information.
6. https://www.ncbi.nlm.nih.gov/pmc/articles/PMC3084045/ Shai Danziger, Jonathan Levav, and Liora Avnaim-Pessoa, "Extraneous factors in judicial decisions," *Proceedings of the National Academy of Science* 2011 Apr 26; 108(17): 6889–6892. A study of eight Israeli judges determining applications for parole found that while on average all judges approved 35% of applications, 65% of applications right after breaks were approved falling down to almost none of the applications considered right before breaks. The conclusion was that the judges were being "distracted" from fairness by feelings like fatigue, hunger and boredom that they insisted were not affecting their judgements.
7. D. Malaspina, C. Corcoran, K. R. Kleinhaus, M. C. Perrin, S. Fennig, D. Nahon, Y. Friedlander, S. Harlap, "Acute maternal stress in pregnancy and schizophrenia in offspring: a cohort prospective study" *BMC Psychiatry* 2008, 8:71 http://www.biomedcentral.com/1471-244X/8/71 Study found that intrauterine stress (in this case during the Israeli Six Days War) contributed to an increased number of emotional deficits after birth, including anxiety, depression, autism and schizophrenia.
8. For a fulsome discussion of the differences and possible collaborations between the faster emotional mind and the slower cognitive mind, see Noble Prize winner Daniel Kahneman, *Thinking Fast and Slow*, New York, NY: Farrar, Strauss and Giroux, 2011.
9. https://www.health.harvard.edu/blog/right-brainleft-brain-right-2017082512222
10. Daniel Goleman, *Working with Emotional Intelligence*, 78–80. New York, NY: Bantam, 2000
11. Shultz, Marjorie M., and Sheldon Zedeck. "Predicting Lawyer Effectiveness: Broadening the Basis for Law School Admission Decisions." *Law and Social Inquiry* 36 (2011)
12. Daniel Goleman, "They've Taken Emotional Intelligence Too Far," *TIME*, November 1, 2011.
13. Larry Richard, "The Psychologically Savvy Leader," LawyerBrain Blog, November 11, 2013, http://www.lawyerbrainblog.com/2013/11/the-psychologically-savvyleader/ .
14. Antoine Bechara et al., "Insensitivity to Future Consequences Following Damage to Human Prefrontal Cortex," *Cognition* 50 (1994): 1–3, 7–15.
15. David Maister, "Are Law Firms Manageable?" *DavidMaister.com*.
16. Beck, Megan, and Barry Libert. "The Rise of AI Makes Emotional Intelligence More Important." *Harvard Business Review*. February 15, 2017.
17. Stein, Steven J., Peter Papadogiannis, Jeremy A. Yip, and Gill Sitarenios.

"Emotional Intelligence of Leaders: A Profile of Top Executives." *Leadership and Organization Development Journal* 30 (2009): 87–101.

18. Groysberg, Boris, and Eliot Sherman. "Baker & McKenzie (A): A New Framework for Talent Management." Harvard Business School, 2007; "Baker & McKenzie (B): A New Framework for Talent Management." Harvard Business School, 2008.
19. Gardner, Heidi. *Smart Collaboration: How Professionals and Their Firms Succeed by Breaking Down Silos*. Boston, MA: Harvard Business Review Press, 2016.
20. An attorney whose practice is devoted entirely to defending disciplinary actions confirms that not recognizing and dealing with emotions like anger and frustration are what put lawyers most at risk for not only a single disciplinary procedure but for multiple ones. Megan Zavieh, "Recovery After Bar Discipline," *Attorney at Work.com*, July 13, 2015, http://www.attorneyatwork.com/recovery-bar-discipline/.
21. Rubin, Robert S., and Ronald E. Riggio. "The Role of Emotional Intelligence in Ethical Decision Making at Work." In *Positive Psychology in Business Ethics and Corporate Responsibility*, edited by Robert A. Giacalone, Carole L. Jurkiewicz, Craig Dunn, 209–229. Charlotte, NC: Information Age, 2005.
22. Yip and Côté, "The Emotionally Intelligent Decision Maker," *Psychological Science*.
23. Freedman, "Case: EQ in the Navy and Marine Corps," *Six Seconds Emotional Intelligence Network*, 14.
24. Robin Wellford Slocum, "An Inconvenient Truth: The Need to Educate Emotionally Competent Lawyers," *Chapman University Law Research Paper*, July 19, 2011, 4.
25. ABA Resolution 302 adopted in February 2018 https://www.americanbar.org/content/dam/aba/images/abanews/mym2018res/302.pdf together with the ABA's *Model Rules of Professional Conduct*, Rule 8.3 and 8.4, revised in August. https://www.americanbar.org/groups/professional_responsibility/publications/model_rules_of_professional_conduct.html.
26. Grewal, Daisy, and Heather A. Davidson, "Emotional Intelligence and Graduate Medical Education." *Journal of the American Medical Association* 10 (2008): 1200–1202.
27. "Ways to Avoid Legal Malpractice, as Claims Rise Industry-Wide," *YourABA*, December, 2016, http://www.americanbar.org/publications/youraba/2016/december-2016/legal-malpractice-claims-are-on-the-rise—but-you-can-takesteps.html. Kara MacKillop and Neil Vidmar, "Legal Malpractice: A Preliminary Inquiry," *First Annual Conference on Empirical Legal Studies Paper*, June 29, 2006. The Canadian agency is the Lawyers' Professional Indemnity Company (LAWPRO).
28. Patrick R. Krill, Ryan Johnson, and Linda Albert, "The Prevalence of Substance Use and Other Mental Health Concerns Among American Attorneys," *Journal of Addiction Medicine* 10 (1): 46–52.

29. C. Stewart Mauny, "The Lawyers' Epidemic: Depression, Suicide and Substance Abuse," *South Carolina Lawyer*, January 2012, 3. https://
30. www.hazeldenbettyford.org/about-us/news-media/press-release/2016-aba-hazelden-release-first-study-attorney-substance-use
31. Brianna Pena, *Falling through the Cracks: A Report on Mental Health at Yale Law School*, New Haven, CT: Yale Law School Mental Health Alliance, 2014.
32. Colin James, Miles Bore, and Susanna Zito, "Emotional Intelligence and Personality as Predictors of Psychological Well-Being," *Journal of Psychoeducational Assessment* 30 (4): 425–38.
33. See Mayo Clinic Staff, "Stress Symptoms: Effects on Your Body and Behavior," Mayo Clinic, http://www.mayoclinic.org/healthy-lifestyle/stress-management/in-depth/stress-symptoms/art-20050987.
34. Elissa Epel, et al., "Can Meditation Slow Rate of Cellular Aging? Cognitive Stress, Mindfulness, and Telomeres," *Annals of the New York Academy of Sciences* 1172 (2009): 34–53.
35. Feng-Jen, Tsai, Wei-Lun Huang, and Chang-Chuan Chan. "Occupational Stress and Burnout of Lawyers." *Journal of Occupational Health* 51 (2009): 443–450.
36. Judy Martin, "Workplace Stress Is Curveball Lobbed at Employee Emotional Intelligence," *Forbes Online*, November 19, 2012, http://www.forbes.com/sites/work-in-progress/2012/11/19/workplace-stress-is-curveballlobbed-at-employee-emotional-intelligence/.
37. Diane Coutu, "The Science of Thinking Smarter: A Conversation with Brain Expert John J. Medina," *Harvard Business Review*, May, 2008, 51-52; "How Does Stress Influence Bad Decision-Making?" *European Commission: Community Research and Development Information Service*, http://cordis.europa.eu/news/rcn/31097_en.html.
38. Robert M. Yerkes and John D. Dodson, "The Relation of the Strength of Stimulus to Rapidity of Habit Formation," *Journal of Comparative Neurology and Psychology* 18 (1908): 459–82.
39. Maria Platsidou and Layla Salman, "The Role of Emotional Intelligence in Predicting Burnout and Job Satisfaction of Greek Lawyers," *International Journal of Law, Psychology and Human Life* 1 (2012): 13–22.
40. Gerald Matthews et al., "Emotional Intelligence, Personality, and Task-Induced Stress," *Journal of Experimental Psychology: Applied* 12 (2006): 96–107.
41. Saklofske et al., "Relationships of Personality, Affect, Emotional Intelligence and Coping with Student Stress and Academic Success: Different Patterns of Association for Stress and Success," *Learning and Individual Differences*, 256.
42. Breslau, Jill, and Susan Daicoff. "The Illicit Relationship of Lawyers and Emotion." *Cutting Edge Law*, September 1, 2008, http://cuttingedgelaw.com/content/illicit-relationship-lawyers-and-emotion.

Chapter 5:
Lessons learned in data analytics

By Melaina Fireman, senior manager of business intelligence and database services at Goodwin Procter LLP

The implementation of formal business intelligence (BI)/data analytics strategies at law firms continues to increase, with data governance and data visualization dashboards playing a significant role. But where does one begin this process? Why do so many BI initiatives fail? Which best practices ensure BI success? Two points are key: (i) understanding that BI initiatives have maturity levels, and (ii) since technology is typically the easiest part of the implementation, it is important to concentrate on people and processes. Most industries are still early in the process of adopting BI strategies, and legal is no exception. To help with these efforts, we are sharing some lessons learned while implementing a formal BI strategy, a growing enterprise data warehouse (EDW), and self-service data visualization platform.

We initially focused our efforts on including data governance when developing an EDW and a data dictionary. We concurrently deployed a data visualization platform that allowed for the development of interactive dashboards to support business analysis. Flexible development techniques on smaller projects helped us initiate quick wins, gain feedback and make improvements. This generated momentum to develop visual analytic solutions for financial analysis, litigation intelligence, business development, human resources, legal recruiting, diversity, program management, client and matter analysis, among other areas.

Our data analysis strategy focused on people and processes along with four specific components, which are discussed in greater detail below:

1. Management;
2. Requirements;
3. Design and deployment; and
4. Support and utilization.

By partnering with business owners throughout the firm and empowering business analysts with best practices, training and support, we are continuing to strengthen a data-driven culture on our BI journey.

Management

Data governance is key to successfully implementing BI services. To help address data quality issues, applying standard labels and validating data management best practices will help optimize the implementation. Data sources are governed for verified providers versus unauthorized custom data sets. As exciting as predictive analytics and AI solutions are, a strong BI foundation is necessary for any environment. An EDW, along with a data dictionary to document data model details, will help developers understand data origins, including ownership and security requirements.

But who owns the data? When combining data that has not been combined before, there needs to be shared accountability, with IT and other business departments taking ownership. This challenging dynamic requires leadership support, transparency and coordination throughout.

Formal data governance policies provide guidance for implementing BI services. Key sponsors throughout the firm, with a strong understanding of BI services, can support existing governance policies and review project requests to determine appropriate priorities. Before starting the formal process, we knew that we would need to address different data with the same name and the same data with different names. Continuous review and centralized management during the process is critical.

Requirements

Without basic requirements, where does one begin? Centralized BI services and formal request processes help business leaders determine initial requirements that can be used for evaluation purposes. We work with our business areas to support their needs and use cases to help determine if a BI service is the optimal solution. While data visualization may be the appropriate solution for most data analysis, it is not right for all. The potential technical options, data quality, timing, resources and priorities all factor into the BI service review.

Once the BI services request is approved, complete detailed requirements can be gathered as necessary. A project may call for new data sets for the EDW and/or data visualizations. Requirements may change, and proper project planning is essential for change management.

Maintaining a clear and supportable warehouse architecture is important as ETL processes are added, updated or removed. Different perspectives and timings of data are necessary to support the BI services, including annual, quarterly, monthly and daily updates. We have developed supporting schema within the EDW to support these distinctions.

Developers must have strong knowledge of data warehousing, business requirements and technical expertise in advanced BI tools. As new ETL processes are developed, the data dictionary can be updated to capture all details within the EDW. Being able to test and review code is key to the process. We continue to evaluate different BI tools to automate processes, monitor infrastructure and enhance BI services throughout the environment.

Design and deployment

While implementing the EDW, we deployed a self-service data visualization platform to provide business analysts the ability to create the dashboards. Our support model is to provide centralized services while empowering those who know the data best to develop the visual analysis to support the business. Our BI community continues to grow, share and learn best practices, improving all BI services.

Standards are an essential component of data governance. In addition to the standard policies and processes for BI services and requests, we continue to apply firm-wide branding on BI services to have a more standard look and feel of dashboards and reports.

Data quality helps support the standards applied. Some dashboards don't even get started due to poor data quality. The EDW and new and existing dashboards are constantly reviewed for data quality, with owners responsible for data quality in the visualizations, and with shared owners undertaking shared review.

Who should have access to the data? ETL development, data visualization development and data access require different levels of security. We continually review best practice solutions and business requirements for each BI service. One lesson we have learned, though, is that even if possible to apply strict security, it doesn't always mean one should. When trying to leverage similar data for multiple types of analysis, different sets of security requirements may conflict.

We have developed different sets of BI groups to support security in multiple ways. Security is a significant component reviewed at the start of any BI service and implemented as needed. It requires continuous review throughout the implementation.

Support and utilization

Along with internal support, we leverage external professional services and expertise, extending resources, training and support as needed. The BI community provides strong support and shares appropriate BI services, tools and resources, and best practices.

We track usage of BI services to determine proper usage and access. We monitor system resources to maintain and continually improve performance. The business owners of the data continually track usage for their BI services and determine next steps based on user feedback.

While we are still early in our BI journey, our strategic vision is to add value to the business through data analytics and to improve decision-making throughout our firm. Our BI services, resources and environment grow as we learn more about implementing best practices and optimal solutions in support of our firm's business strategy.

Chapter 6:
Four ways to use data and analytics for business development

By Michelle Murray, chief marketing officer at Cahill Gordon & Reindel LLP

According to an overwhelming number of studies from legal market consultants, law firm revenue growth was flat in 2016–2017. The decrease in overall demand for legal billable hours combined with the abundance of new entrants into the legal services market has exacerbated the problem facing law firms. It has never been more important for a law firm to understand their market share and develop a strategic plan to compete.

Due to today's rapidly changing market for legal services, law firms have engaged a myriad of strategies to adapt and compete. One investment many firms are making is in their marketing and business development department. Over the past few years, business development and marketing has become more of a science than an art – largely due to the availability and abundance of data. Litigation and transactional analytics tools allow users to benchmark themselves against their peers, receive alerts about potential new business, and assess litigation and transactions activity by practice area, volume of matters, and significant clients and industries at large. This chapter explores four ways legal professionals can harness big data to better identify both opportunities and competitive risks.

Finding opportunities: becoming the trusted advisor

One consistent piece of client feedback is that in-house counsel wants their lawyers to be a trusted advisor, providing practical advice and not just legal services. To do that, lawyers need to understand how their clients' businesses work, keep abreast of the changes facing their clients' industries, and be aware of the activity of the clients' competition. Assuming a lawyer didn't spend the first part of their career working directly in the industry of their client, they will most likely turn to their business development department to assist them with securing this important intel.

Any marketing professional will tell you that it often seems nearly impossible to get their lawyers to prioritize business development, so streamlining the information is key to success. Many data resources including, but not limited to, providers like Thomson Reuters and BloombergLaw have designed dashboards to assist lawyers with this task. These dashboards can be customized to include a variety of information that provides the viewer everything from up-to-the-minute on company and industry news briefings, litigation alerts and dockets, social media commentary on the company, and intelligence on changes in the company's management structure. Armed with this intel, a lawyer is better positioned to understand the issues facing the client and provide practical solutions.

Client targeting and lead generation

Data and analytics are also widely used in law firm marketing and business development departments for client targeting strategies and lead generation. Many firms are increasing the research function to focus on data integration and have implemented a metrics oriented approach to business development. 2017 even saw a few firms investing in artificial intelligence; however, human resources are still needed to evaluate and properly apply the data produced.

Some firms have a business development team member oversee sourcing leads for the transactional practice to find opportunities for easy touch points with existing clients and target clients. This intelligence can also be used for strategic planning and client meeting prep. The following is a real-life example of this how this information is used.

> Partner A is going to visit an important existing client, a bank who provides financing across a variety of industries. The research you have done shows that your firm, while having loads of experience in this particular industry, has not done any of the work for the client in that industry in the past year. This knowledge gives the partner 1) the ability to show the client they are active in the market and aware of the client's business activities in each industry, and 2) an entrée for the partner to share the firm's extensive experience in the industry in question. Often the client may be unaware of the firm's experience in the industry and this conversation will convert to new work for the firm.

It may seem simplistic, but people do business with people they like. Personality is important, but preparation is also key to success. Similar to most firms, my firm's business development team provides client dossiers to the attorneys to help prepare them for meetings with potential clients. The individual bios – which include work history of the individual(s), where they went to university/college, any volunteer work or other personal intel – help the attorney to better know the prospect and to find common ground. There are some data sources a firm can pay for, but most of what you need is readily available with a simple Google or LinkedIn search.

Next, you will want to create a dossier on the legal work the client has needed over the past five years. This can include both transaction and litigation matters. Since there is so much information available, it is always best to have a conversation with the partner so you can provide targeted information for the meeting.

Creating a transactional dossier might include evaluating the data on reported transactions, market rumors and the alerts that we've set up to monitor company news. Understanding what types of deals are being done, the structure of the deal, the parties involved, and the industry provides our attorneys valuable intel when speaking with their clients and prospects.

When preparing a litigation dossier, the team will dig into each practice area the prospective company has litigation in evaluating the law firms currently serving the prospect, the jurisdictions the matters are in and the judges they appear before. Litigation sources like Thomson's Monitor Suite or BloombergLaw can be reverse engineered to track active plaintiff firms in a particular practice. Keeping clients abreast of litigation facing their competition and providing a solution for avoiding this litigation is extraordinarily valuable.

The rise of the RFP

Under pressure to manage costs, general counsels are pulling resources in-house and increasing their own teams as well as issuing an increased number of requests for proposals (RFP) as they search for alternatives to provide budget certainty.

The benefits of competitive intelligence (CI) tools in responding to RFPs and pitches for prospects are listed below.

CI tools are valuable when evaluating a go/no-go decision – the decision on whether a firm should expend valuable resources to respond to a lengthy RFP. Asking the following questions and evaluating the answers against your own firm's strategy will help in determining the go/no-go:

- What kind of litigation has this company faced?
- What courts are they in?
- What types of transactions do they do?
- Who is providing legal services for each of these practice areas?
- What does the list of providers tell us about the company's legal service purchasing history?

The answers to these questions will tell you if you are geographically positioned to offer the services, can compete on rates, and have the requisite experience.

One of the most important questions you need to answer is what types of matters the prospective client has and what type of service provider is doing the work for them. Knowing what types of litigation and transactional work the prospective client has had, and which law firms are providing the services, will provide insight into whether or not your firm is well-positioned to provide the legal services. For example, you may conclude from the data that your firm is actually *not* a good fit. The company may be using lower cost providers in local markets, or the practices they are most active in don't match up to those offered by the law firm, or the bulk of the matters are in practice areas that don't match up with your firm's specialties.

If the decision to participate in the RFP is a go, you should then dig deeper into the data to find out who they use for different types of work. What else does that information tell you? It could tell you that the client has a panel of "go-to" firms or that the firms the company is currently using charge less and you will have to consider alternative fees or discounts to win business away from the existing providers. The information will also help you to create a case for how your firm differentiates itself from the firm(s) providing the services currently.

Data for firm strategy, benchmarking and resource allocation

Evaluating the data for trends and opportunities is key to building and reviewing the effectiveness of a firm-wide business development strategy. All good business development professionals know it is important for a firm to have a business development strategy; however, it is just as important to track strategic plans along the way. Using data to evaluate the firm's market position in the practice area throughout the established business development plan's timeline, any new entrants to the practice area, and any news allows you to make any necessary corrections to ensure the practice proceeds along the path to success. Here is an example of how the data provided could help a practice group adapt to market conditions and provide an opportunity to succeed:

> The firm's strategic planning committee has set a goal of increasing market share in the capital markets practice by five percent for the calendar year. The plan includes highlighting the firm's extensive experience in debt capital markets to the firm's existing and prospective clients. However, during the year, your research shows that overall economic conditions have changed and/or new laws were recently enacted which make it is less likely that companies will issue new debt in the form on bonds. Since the current plan included growth by representing bond issuers, the firm's leadership will need to adjust the plan and replace this type of work with another service offering if they want to reach their growth goals.

We also use the data to evaluate competitive risks and benchmark the firm's and individual practice area's performance. Tools like BloombergLaw, Debtwire, and Thomson Reuters' LPC provide league tables that specifically outline your firm's performance in a particular practice area. These tables provide great infographics to include in pitch materials. Your research team members can also dig into the databases of Monitor Suite and LCD to further analyze your firm's position in various practice areas. Often you will need to use two tools together to get the full picture. As you analyze the data, remember to look at more than just matter count. While we all know that bringing in new matters is one measure of growth, you need to look at the entire market including your practice's position as a percentage of the market and your growth in terms of your competitors. Imagine the following scenario:

> Research from internal sources (billing and hours reports) shows that your practice area saw a decrease in the number of matters it has worked on year over year. News and intelligence gathered from various resources show that the overall market has contracted significantly.

What does this scenario tell you? Should you blindly accept that it's a down market and assume there will be fewer matters being handled by your firm? While that is clearly the case, you should dig a little deeper and look at the past five years of data to get a better picture of your firm's position in this particular practice area. Further evaluation might show that your firm actually owns a much larger percentage of the practice area in down markets. It will also give you an idea of the maturity of the practice area, how many of the participants you are serving, and – of the ones you are serving – how many of their matters you advised on.

The final step is deciding what to do with the information you have gathered. The strategic business decisions a firm's management team and practice leadership makes with the newly gleaned competitive intelligence may range from plans to find new prospective clients to pitch, increasing panel participation through an increase in RFP participation, to allocating the business development time, to strengthening the existing relationships or – depending on the culture of the firm – all of the above. This intel is also good for evaluating internal resource allocation. Management may need to reallocate headcount in departments or hire additional staff to assist an area seeing a surge in growth.

The combination of additional in-house resources with the advancements in technology and other tools to collect data has really changed the landscape in the competitive intelligence arena, and positions marketing and business development teams to play an even bigger role in sourcing opportunities for lawyers.

Chapter 7: A legal data analytics journey

By Kesney Fontes, data analytics manager at WilmerHale

A brief description of the modern law firm data reporting needs

A large law firm handles tens of thousands or hundreds of thousands of active matters on a daily basis. There are thousands of new matters being created every month, with thousands of time keepers contributing to such matters. In addition to this, there are hundreds of partners who bring to the firm their portfolio of matters and clients and who have the responsibility to maintain their individual and the firm's relationships with such clients. The partners are members of departments and practice groups. A smaller number of such partners manages those departments and practice groups, with separate strategical agendas and goals. All these individual contributors have their carrier goals and, further, they collaborate towards departmental and overall firm strategies and set of objectives.

An analytics platform, in a law firm, bears the task to serve all of the above in their day-to-day efforts, while managing individual matters, practice groups, departments and the firm. It is often a challenge to negotiate between each separate and frequently conflicting goal. An effective reporting platform must be flexible to adjust to individual groups and at the same time must be standardized to be manageable and to foster a common firm culture. It must provide close to real-time reporting of current state of matters and must answer the consumer's questions, with the proper level of information disclosure to each level of the firm administration.

Every functioning organization already have data consumers asking questions, and data owners answering those questions. That dialog certainly already exists. The goal in implementing a data analytics platform is to make the existing dialog more efficient. Our journey was a synergetic effort of those organizations and individuals that were already fulfilling our consumer's needs. Our effort achieved more efficient and standardized access to the data that billing and supervising attorneys needed to manage their matters, department and practice group chairs needed to manage their groups, and myriad other information workers needed to do their job.

To build or to buy

One of the first questions that we had to answer was whether we would build or buy a solution. I am personally a big proponent of the buy option. The benefit of buying is the quick time to market, from the time you start the effort to the time you start to reap the benefits of your investment. The challenge with buying is that it needs to be flexible enough to adjust to the needs of the firm, various departments, various practice groups, partners, timekeepers, and so on. The challenge of building such a solution is that you must have the right technical skill set to create and maintain it; it also can take too long until you start to realize the benefits on your investments.

In our case, we chose to build. We had the right skill set at hand, and it was easy to identify that the available products in the market were still struggling with the ever-changing requirements of modern matter management in a law firm. The decision was therefore not hard to make; building our own solution enabled us to attain a lot more flexibility. Finally, the Microsoft Analysis Services tabular platform and PowerBI visualization software was just good enough that we felt confident in moving forward with building our solution.

It took a village

The initiative of creating a matter management solution had been simmering for almost two years.

Very early in the process, we were able to recognize the importance of creating alignment of the vision and processes across the firm. There was a need to have a cross-functional (practice management, information services and financial services) and streamlined group, focused on delivery and continuing the communication with stakeholders (partners and management).

We believe if any of these individual groups had taken upon themselves to implement a siloed solution, it would not have been as successful as it has been. We adopted an iterative process, where small deliverables were identified and developed, followed by a very quick and focused feedback loop. These iterations sometimes would go on for 10 to 20 cycles in the process of completing one report. Some of the iterations took one hour, others took a week; however, all of them were a very collaborative process.

Initially nobody involved was 100 percent dedicated to the effort. It took over a year to have the first fully dedicated resources. Practice management first and then information services recognized the importance of data analytics and consequently created a new department that was fully resourced.

The effort to develop our first data warehouse was staffed internally, and it took about two months for the first reports to start being distributed to the partners managing matters. We started producing reports while continuously improving and augmenting the data warehouse. The key was to demonstrate value while building a solid data analytics foundation, as most data warehouse initiatives fail because they take too long to build, often without any immediate and obvious benefits.

We tried to keep our stakeholders interested and excited by involving them in the process. Practice management and financial services identified their requirements based on existing reports and interviews of partners and matter teams. Information services, at that time, needed to expand the data warehouse in order to address data gaps. Financial services validated the accuracy of the data and practice management initiated a pilot group for each report. Each report was an enabler of improvements of existing processes. This recipe was repeated and proved very successful.

The technical solution

We leverage Microsoft technology, despite having looked at multiple data analytics platforms; however, our timing was lucky, as the Microsoft Analysis Services tabular platform was becoming stable and PowerBI was starting to impress developers and consumers during our period of trial and implementation. During our first two years we focused purely on SSIS for the ETL (extract, transform and load) process; this is the process data that is extracted from the transactional systems and transformed into a data format more appropriate for reporting, which is then loaded into the SQL server engine that would be queried by the reports. All reports were developed through Microsoft SQL Server Reporting Services. We needed two homegrown applications used for the delivery of the reports. The first one developed was to assist with the creation of subscriptions of reports and delivery of such subscriptions. We decided to build our own solution, because the out-of-the-box option included in SSRS (data driven subscriptions) did not allow multiple reports to be delivered with the same email; it also didn't enable reports to be embedded into the email body with a second report attached at the same time. Eventually, we created a second application for matter teams to self-service and run reports whenever needed.

After the first two years we initiated the development of a Microsoft Analysis Services database, which is key for an extremely fast data aggregation. The tabular model of the Analysis Service is the server-side version of the same engine used in the PowerBI applications. That was our first exposure to DAX ("Data Analyzes Expressions"), which is the scripting language used to implement your data model within the Analysis Server Service tabular mode. DAX is fascinating. It is different from TSQL, which is used to develop queries against the relational database; it is also very powerful, and a nice evolution in how a developer interacts with data in the Microsoft ecosystem.

In the last two years, we have gone through three iterations of our main data cube. We have updated our SSAS servers multiple times to take advantage of new features. This flexibility was paramount for our success, and I believe the decision to home-build our solution was very fortunate in affording us the required flexibility.

Finally, the monthly releases of PowerBI enhancements have bridged the initial gaps and provided a platform that empower our financial services and practice management to create their own reports with minimal assistance from information services. This has allowed information services to focus on maintaining and enhancing the underlying data framework and data model, with a conservative number of developers.

The business value

A large law firm, like WilmerHale, produces hundreds of thousands of billable hours by thousands of timekeepers every month, on behalf of a large number of clients. Real-time data is paramount for managing each matter efficiently, for keeping each client informed, and for achieving the goals of each practice group, department, and the firm.

A billing attorney can effectively track hours worked on their matters and take appropriate actions when necessary, as well as keeping the client informed in a timely manner of actual versus budget. The weekly or daily delivery of our reports provide the right level of information that each matter team requires. Our reports are providing real-time and accurate information for the decision-makers, which empowers them to make intelligent and prompt choices that are influenced and informed by concrete data sets.

Our legal project management services assist on the management of large and complex matters. The legal project managers are leveraging the reports to provide timely answers and recommendations on the intricate nuances of leverage, write-downs, works in progress, accounts receivables, write-offs, billings, collections, and so on.

These reports are also used by our pricing group to analyze and provide budgets and to manage actuals against those budgets.

With the power of the data cube and the roll-up and drill-down capabilities of the visualization tool, the aggregation of structured data empowers each firm management level to see across their area of responsibility, from firm management down to matter level information.

The future

A data platform requires constant care and feeding. Maintenance of the technical solution following the constant patches of servers and applications and the upgrade of our source systems carries direct impact that needs to be kept coordinated and in harmony. Each consumer group is always changing and evolving, with new requirements emerging frequently. The village that created this solution must continue to work in tight collaboration in order to maintain it.

The data science world is evolving at an incredibly accelerated pace. New advances quickly develop from nice-to-haves to existential necessities. For many clients, such necessities are critical requirements. Moving from descriptive reporting into advance analytics is our natural next step. In the future, I anticipate data projects with a focus on internal process improvements.

Data is becoming more available and the legal worker is becoming more data literate, with powerful data visualization tools consuming a wide scope of data available on our data framework.

Incorporation of external data, which will become available for purchase, will build data bridges to internal information. This path will bring significant competitive advantage to both the firms which consume and the data aggregators that sell such data sets.

Finally, the future that is already here is the empowerment of financial services, practice management and legal project management to become versed in creating their own reports, without the need of direct involvement of information services.

Chapter 8:

Mind over matter: how to promote the necessity of business analytics in a resistant culture

By Paige D Keith, chief financial officer at Hawkins Parnell Thackston & Young, LLP

Business intelligence tools have been instrumental in analyzing historical and current data to assist law firms in both business and operational decisions. However, many firms have been making successful decisions without the use of business intelligence tools for years. Some law firm leaders may say they have always relied on "gut instincts", but sometimes the analysis may suggest that "gut instincts" are not always the best measure for decision making. However, firms that discount intuition may be making mistakes too. This chapter explores why law firms rely on intuition and the consequences of discounting both business analytics and intuition in their decision-making process.

What is intuition, and is it a business intelligence tool itself?

In 1952, Bill Allen, the CEO of Boeing, went before his board and pitched the idea for Boeing to produce commercial jet planes. Boeing had long provided military jets as a leading defense contractor, but Allen had a "hunch" that by building a commercial jet, he could meet a demand that did not even exist yet for fast and efficient global passenger transportation. The costs of the project, he explained to his board, were larger than the value of the company at that time. The tools most commonly used in business decision making all should have guided the board to say no. The NPV (Net Present Value) of the project was negative; the future demand was uncertain; there were no assured sales or even assured interest; and foreign competitors already had a head start. However, the board said yes because of Bill Allen's prior success in large risky projects. The resulting success story of Bill Allen and his "hunch" about the 707 might be a great story in the power of trusting instinct over rudimentary business intelligence and decision making. However, Bill Allen was not an inexperienced business leader who convinced the board of a multimillion dollar company to take a gamble. He was an experienced leader who used prior knowledge (historical data), competitive intelligence (he visited the British competitor de Havilland to scope out the "Comet" – a jet transport plane that was in production), and reliance on company resources (he asked his executives and engineers about the feasibility, costs and changes that would need to happen) to make a business decision that might save a company whose viability relied on the US going to war. The point is that the board's decision to risk the company may have been based on its CEO's intuition, but Allen used business intelligence to support his intuition, allowing the board some comfort in its gamble. By the way, Bill Allen was not an engineer who worked his way through the management ranks at Boeing. Bill Allen was a lawyer.

Practice leaders and law firm owners often find themselves in similar situations as Bill Allen. As lawyers they rely on past experience, knowledge of law, jurisdictions, case studies, judges and jury pools to make legal decisions when helping clients. However, for the most part they are not data analysts or financial planners, and yet they are also put into positions of making business decisions from pricing to mergers and acquisitions. For many years, the business intelligence they had – historical data, prior success and failures and "gut instincts" – often led to very successful business endeavors, sound decisions and good client relationships. Some argue that intuition has served them well, as evidenced by decades of success prior to the intervention of spreadsheets, dashboards, knowledge management systems, and other current business intelligence tools. Bruce Henderson, founder of Boston Consulting Group, called intuition "the subconscious integration of all the experiences, condition and knowledge of a lifetime, including the cultural and emotional biases of that lifetime". Today's business tools arguably do the same thing, just on a conscious and purposeful level – they mine and consolidate experiences and knowledge, but on a much greater scale than a single mind. It is true that they do lack the ability to mine cultural and emotional biases, which is why both sides – those who rely on intuition and those who rely on physical business intelligence tools – are necessary in the decision-making process.

The dangers of relying solely on "gut instincts"

Let us consider a possible scenario: lateral partner acquisition.

In hoping to expand its geographical presence, a law firm heavily recruits lateral partner candidates in major cities. As part of its due diligence, it requires reasonable financial and historical performance data from all candidates. It performs multiple proformas and multiple partners interview each candidate. The firm narrows its choice to two candidates in one major city. One candidate has a strong existing book of business, but is relatively unknown to the partners in the firm. His production and performance over the last three years is strong and consistent and is growing slowly. He has a strong market presence in the city. The proforma shows a return on investment by his second year. Some partners think he fits well with the existing culture, while others just don't agree.

The other candidate has been involved in a few cases with some of the partners. He has a smaller book of business, but it has grown rapidly in the last three years and he strongly feels that he is on the verge of obtaining more business that would end up placing the firm in a strong position in a new market. A proforma not including the prospective business shows a return on investment at the current growth rate by his fifth year. The proforma with the prospective business shows a return on investment by his second year and more revenue than the first candidate. The partners who had cases with him convince a few of the partners that he fits well with the firm.

A law firm that is weary of analytics and has always relied on "gut instincts" may choose the second candidate based on familiarity and history and take a larger financial risk, discrediting the first proforma in favor of the second one to support its position, although it is based on only prospective business. The scenario above is simplified greatly. Opening an office based on lateral acquisitions in another city is a complex decision, with a lot of factors needing to be examined. However, it's the complexity of the decision that may lead law firm leaders to rely on their gut instinct more than the business analysis and even apply biases to the analysis to support their position. In the *HBR* May 2003 article "Don't Trust Your Gut", its author, Eric Bonabueay, notes: "Detached from rigorous analysis, intuition is a fickle and undependable guide – it is as likely to lead to disaster as to success…The more options you have to evaluate, the more data you have to weigh, and the more unprecedented the challenges you face, the less you rely on instinct and more on reason and analysis." He goes on to further note that "we're irrationally influenced by the first information we receive on a particular subject – it becomes, as decision researchers put it, the 'anchor' that determines and distorts how we process all subsequent data." In the scenario above, the familiarity of successfully working with the lawyer in the past influences the partner's rational view of the analytics.

Law firm leaders may be hesitant to rely on business intelligence for fear of truth and accountability. In the May 31, 2016 article in Forbes, "How to Overcome the Three Fears that Undermine Data Analytics", Meta S. Brown writes: "When you commit to measurement and testing, you're also committing to admit that some of your decisions go wrong. That's a risk many executives aren't willing to take." In the lateral partner acquisition scenario above, it is easier for law firm managers to place blame on circumstance than on an initial poor decision. "He really was a nice guy – it's not his fault that the business didn't come. It was the right decision – we were just unlucky that the business didn't come like he promised", they may say." When Bryan Cave started implementing BI in its business decision and analysis, it had to expel fears that the tools would be used against lawyers and staff as a performance report by constantly promoting the positive aspects: serving clients and managing projects.[1]

Law firms may also discount analytics when they don't support the traditional culture or business practices of the firm, leading them to solely lean on experience and intuition. Business analytics and intelligence – in its primary purpose to increase profitability – may expose unprofitable books of business or unprofitable clients and/or staffing structures. In traditional business models, when costs increase to a point that a business is losing money by producing the same product, it may choose to discontinue that use, especially if the loss is inevitable overtime. However, in law firms, the highest cost centers are its revenue generators. They are humans, colleagues, family and friends. Law firms have long rewarded loyalty and longevity as well as skill through compensation. Today's pricing pressures continue to reduce the margin at which some lawyers are working, especially those at higher compensation brackets. Law firms are hesitant to freeze or reduce salaries for skilled associates and partners that are unable to demand higher prices because of loyalty and fear of losing not only revenue generators but also friends. Some law firms may be willing to keep an unprofitable client because of a long relationship on false hopes of obtaining more business and fears of losing revenue despite the cost of doing business with that client. Yielding to the firm culture and its loyalty in these circumstances can lead to irreversible expectations that create financial uncertainty, resulting in defections and loss of profitable clients and attorneys.

One last reason law firm management discounts analytics is because they may not understand them. The traditional tools of business decision making – expected value analysis, options, decision trees, and so on – are often foreign to lawyers. Statistics and data accuracy can be complex in their descriptions; too much can quickly become uninteresting. But lawyers do understand experience and intuition. It serves them well in their chosen profession. It's easy to rely on anecdotal evidence to support decisions, and we are told from childhood to never ignore our instincts. Understanding analytics, what they mean, the assumptions and constraints of data, and the multiple facets of the consequences of each decision requires time and willingness to accept their validity. However, if understood, business intelligence and analytics can serve a much greater purpose than operational decision making. The science of data analytics is a huge part of today's litigation and legal world – from medicinal trials to patent mining to jury research. The ability to understand these gives lawyers a leg up in their practices as well as in firm leadership. In fact, several law schools including MSU, are offering courses in quantitative analysis.

The dangers of a sole reliance on BI data

Another firm may select the first partner candidate in the scenario above in acquiring lateral partners, despite the concerns of some of the partners that the candidate "didn't feel right" because the candidate presented a strong book of business. The firm's willingness to discount the "feeling" may create resentment and create a self-fulfilling prophesy, dooming the candidate.

The essence of decision-making in business is that there are so many complex scenarios that create multiple analysis to be required. In instances where time is important, relying on time consuming research and analysis may not be possible. In Malcom Gladwell's book, *Blink*, he argues that the brain is able to process information and perform instant calculations in a short amount of time – that generally leads to correct decisions. He admits the fallacies associated with this, but generally concludes that in a "blink", the brain knows even if it doesn't know why. In the *HBR* article "When It's Safe to Rely on Intuition (and When It's Not)" from April 2015, Consson Chou Locke notes that "there is simply too much information coming at us from all directions and too many decisions that we need to make from moment to moment, to think every single one through a long and detailed analysis… While this can sometimes backfire, in many cases intuition is a perfectly fine shortcut."

She goes onto point out that intuition is helpful only certain conditions, with the most important condition being expertise. In the scenario of lateral partner acquisition – where partners who have been with the firm for a long time and have seen partners come and go and know what type of practice or partner fits – the "feeling" of those partners should not be discounted.

One problem that mid-size law firms face in using business intelligence tools and data analytics is that, without strong data governance policies, analysis can be limited by the validity and consistency of the data. Recognizing the limitations of a small and inconsistent data sources doesn't negate the usefulness of business intelligence, but it may require relying on intuition and gut instinct to complete holes or contradictions in data. Even with the presence of good data, bad decisions can still be made because humans still make decisions. The *HBR* article from "Good Data Won't Guarantee Good Decisions" from April 2012 argues that "investments in analytics can be useless, even harmful, unless employees can incorporate data into complex decision making."

Multiple leadership books provide examples and beautiful stories of success where people either relied on their gut to make decisions or proved their intuition. If intuition is really a brain's compilation of data, historical events and experiences, it becomes a valuable resource and tool in decision-making, doing the same thing that business intelligence tools do on a broader scale.

Mind and matter – using judgment and data to drive decision making?

Business intelligence tools designed for data analytics, specifically those for law firm use, are getting better and faster, analyzing the complexities and multiple scenarios to help provide strong data on which firms can base decisions, where before time limits required them to rely on those "gut instincts". However, intuition is based on historical knowledge, and law firm leaders' experience should not be discounted, especially where culture may counter the results of an analysis. "Good Data Won't Guarantee Good Decisions", from April 2012, reports on a study that the employees best equipped to make good decisions "effectively balance judgment and analysis, possess strong analytic skills and listen to others' opinions but are willing to dissent. They're the kind of data-savvy workers every company should try to cultivate". In other words, good decisions by law firm leaders are a result of both business intelligence and intuition.

Reference

1. Diann Daniel, "How a Global Law Firm Used Business Intelligence to Fix Customer Billing Woes", *CIO*, January 8 2008.

Chapter 9:
Design Thinking and the *why* of BI

By John Alber, futurist at the Institute for the Future of Law Practice

Change or die

The decision to implement BI doesn't always get the scrutiny it needs. And the name may have as much to do with it as anything. "Business Intelligence", after all, is such a delectable term, ripe and full, suited to almost any business setting. Take a budget meeting, for example. When asked why you want to spend a half million dollars on a piece of software and still more on implementation and staff, "business intelligence" is an ideal rejoinder. Just serve it up and wait for the cash to follow.

Because who doesn't want to be intelligent about their business? And that desire seems a sufficient end in itself, something that forecloses all further inquiry. So, what better than spending a sizable chunk on BI and throwing up a dashboard – or 20 – as a means of being more... intelligent about your business? Because, obviously, BI means smart.

Beware the obvious. More than most technology investments in business, buying a BI suite needs careful thought at the start, and ongoing attention as it is used. In law, we have only to look around to see why. Many firms have by now invested in CRM and other BI software and staff. But how many can claim to have transformed their relationships with clients or dramatically improved their businesses as a result? Can you name one? Is the delivery of legal services any different as a result?

Truth is, most BI investments are wasted. They produce dashboard eye candy alright. But they don't truly add the kind of intelligence that changes a business's course. And the reason for that is an almost complete lack of attention to the question of why we seek business intelligence in the first place.

We buy BI to *survive*. Today's highly dynamic global marketplace grinds through businesses faster than at any time in the history of business. The average lifespan of a Fortune 500 corporation now may be as little as 15 years. And smaller businesses die sooner. Smaller businesses like law firms?

You would think so. In Big Law, the principle of *stare decisis* applies far beyond legal precedent and well into business practice. Lawyers, we often say, are resistant to change, and perhaps even inimical to it. *Status quo* forever!

So, as Fortune 500 lifespans move from 50 years to as little as 15, why haven't we seen a Big Law extinction event? Perhaps it's because of the insulating effect of the billable hour. That cost-plus business model excuses a lot of obliviousness – and disguises mortality.

But, notwithstanding the billable hour hiatus Big Law has enjoyed, all businesses begin to die the day they are founded, even law firms. And the highest mortality rate arises in those businesses that resolutely stick to their business plans no matter the circumstances. Like Big Law.

Peter Drucker, perhaps the most esteemed management theorist in all of modern business, explains why in his book *Management Challenges for the 21st Century*:

> *"[I]n a period of upheaval, such as the one we are living in, change is the norm. To be sure, it is painful and risky, and above all, it requires a great deal of very hard work. But unless an organization sees that its task is to lead change, that organization – whether a business, a university, or a hospital – will not survive. In a period of rapid structural change the only organizations that survive are the 'change leaders.' It is therefore a central 21st-century challenge for management that its organization become a change leader."*

So, Drucker says, the lesson of businesses in all sectors is *change or die*. Adaptation assures survival.

In the wake of the Great Recession, law *is* in a period of great upheaval. And radical change is rampant, both in the economics of practice and in the how of accomplishing everyday tasks. But that change in the how of practice is not coming from inside the profession; rather almost all significant innovation emanates from outside traditional firms.

Services such as RocketLawyer and LegalZoom are redefining the infrastructure for the delivery of legal services. Virtual entities such as Axiom, Counsel on Call and VLP are reformulating what it means to be a firm. Blockchain-based technologies are restructuring that most basic of legal instrumentalities – the contract – and offering up electronic contracts that are lawyerless, smart and self-enforcing. Alternate

dispute resolution services are springing up to remedy the cost, delay and unfairness inherent in an overloaded court system. And all of this is clearly just a beginning. Watson and his yet-to-be-thought-up companions are waiting in the wings.

From all of this, it's clear that law firms of all sizes will have to change too. We've seen that lesson over and over in other industries. Law firms that don't change will get Kodaked, or Blackberried, or Blockbustered. They'll simply fade into irrelevance as the market redefines itself around them. Because *change or die* is the way all business works.

But change how?

Here is where BI pays dividends. Because BI's sweet spot lies precisely in answering questions like "How should we change?" BI is a compass for the business. It helps define the path toward change.

Unfortunately, just buying BI software doesn't automatically create a compass. Someone has to decide what questions to ask, questions that pave the way for change. BI software sometimes comes equipped to ask certain questions. "Are we profitable?" for example. Or even "Where are we profitable?" All it takes is little wiring into existing enterprise systems and those questions can begin to be answered.

And, of course, profitability is one of the core inquiries of any successful business. But just how well does profitability or unprofitability answer the question "Where shall we change?" It may begin an inquiry, but it by no means ends it.

Design thinking discipline

So if BI software can't answer the most important questions right out of the box, how do business leaders in general and BI analysts in particular begin to know what questions to ask to lay in a path for change? How do they even know where to start?

Just as there is a discipline to parsing data, understanding data distributions and undertaking regression analyses, there is also a discipline to designing or redesigning a business. And that is exactly what BI undertakes to do. When we ask what needs to change, we are by definition designing something to take the place of the *status quo*.

And there is a discipline to design that we can make use of in asking these fundamental questions. Over the past several decades, businesses have begun to notice that professionals in design fields – architects, urban planners, industrial designers, and other "creative" types – solve problems in a fundamentally different way than scientists, businesspeople and lawyers. They exert just as much discipline as more conventional analytical thinkers, but often wind up in very different, and much more productive, places. Design Thinking, as it has come to be called, is a translation of the methods used by the most successful designers into language that can be applied in other settings.

Design Thinking is a catchy name, but a little misleading, given our understanding of the term "design." When we speak of design, we often attach an article to it, referring to "a" particular design as being beautiful, or elegant. The smooth metallic surface and radiused edges of the iPhone, for example, fit that understanding of design. In that sense, design refers to a particular physical aesthetic and it seems to fall far outside realms like business and law.

But design is also a process, a methodology used to arrive at a superior end state. And it goes far beyond the physical aesthetics of product creation to encompass the entire user experience associated with a product or service.

As attractive as the iPhone's physical design was, the revolution it spawned had much more to do with how users interacted with a wide range of services, from telephony, to email to music to photography and videography.

And to get to *that* required a most extraordinary kind of inquiry. Because had you asked conventional phone users whether they needed something like the iPhone, they would have said no. They might have quarreled with this or that bit of functionality in their phones, but they were not asking for iPhones.

To get to the iPhone, something else had to happen during the design. This "something else," this way of inquiring that is so different from the way in which businesspeople and lawyers typically approach problems, can prove revolutionary when applied to business problems. And, more particularly, it can serve as an underpinning for the ever-present BI questions: "What shall we measure?" and "What shall we change?"

Empathy?

At the core of Design Thinking is something utterly outside the toolset given lawyers in law school and businesspeople in business school – empathy. Empathy goes beyond simply trying to understand a problem. It asks you to put yourself in the shoes of the person who will use your product or service, and to try to understand that person in ways that transcend logic, that draw upon intuition and emotion as well.

Design Thinking recognizes the first-level importance of the emotional content of a successful design. When we think of traditional value propositions, we often bring to mind some emotionless notion of utility. This product or service will accomplish a certain thing. Lawyers think like that. We will provide you with advice, and it will be correct. BI analysts think like that too. We will tell you your billing speed and collection speed and it will be correct.

But the most successful designs go beyond mere utility. If you buy a Tesla, the automaker promises that you will receive the safest transportation in the world, that you will be transported in a sumptuous surround, that you will feel pampered, affluent, and intelligent. In other words, the design of a Tesla is loaded with emotional content. So too with the iPhone. Its hip exclusivity is as much a part of the design as its elegant user interface. All of the best designs are founded first on human considerations.

Clients have been telling us for years that they want more than utility in their law firms. One of the most common complaints about lawyers is that they take no time to understand their clients' businesses. That complaint certainly relates to the utility of advice – abstract advice is less valuable than that given in a specific business context. But the complaint also has just as much emotional content as a "you don't pay enough attention to me" statement in any other human relationship.

That untapped resource, the as yet unasked questions that open up the workings of our clients' businesses, presents an extraordinary opportunity for BI. Helping lawyers understand their clients' businesses, or even better, helping clients themselves better understand their businesses, represents the foremost opportunity of BI in law.

Bringing empathy to BI

So, what might it look like to begin applying Design Thinking to the question of how to use BI to improve the delivery of legal services?

First, let's get this out of the way. There's some work involved. As you might expect with any discipline, there is a good deal of structure to Design Thinking and a real learning curve. And you'll need to work your way up that curve. A good way to get started is to use the resources compiled by the Stanford Design School, one of the leading proponents of Design Thinking in the technology sector. Stanford's D School is especially influential on designs emerging from Silicon Valley. The D School's *Bootcamp Bootleg* will get you off and running in applying Design Thinking to your work.

But before we do all that work can we test run what empathy-based design feels like? Sure! One of the most approachable answers to that question comes from Warren Berger, who in the Harvard Business Review's *The Four Phases of Design Thinking* describes the sort of mental states that arise during Design Thinking. Berger's observations, arrived at after consulting with and watching closely as over a hundred designers did their work, nicely deconstruct empathy and summarize the ensuing design steps. To quote Berger, when you do Design Thinking successfully, you do four things:

> *"Question. If you spend any time around designers, you quickly discover this about them: They ask, and raise, a lot of questions. Often this is the starting point in the design process, and it can have a profound influence on everything that follows. Many of the designers I studied … talked about the importance of asking 'stupid questions' – the ones that challenge the existing realities and assumptions in a given industry or sector. The persistent tendency of designers to do this is captured in the joke designers tell about themselves. How many designers does it take to change a light bulb? Answer: Does it have to be a light bulb?"*

Berger notes that it can be particularly difficult to ask those "stupid" questions, because they can make the questioner seem naïve. And he wasn't talking about lawyers, who may be more skeptical and cynical than the average business person. Lawyers, he might agree, constitute the Design Thinking acid test. But skeptics and cynics or not, Berger emphasizes that the telling question is the heart of Design Thinking. So summon your courage and get to the soul of the matter. Be willing to ask even the most fundamental questions, ones as fundamental as "What business are we in?"

> *"Care. Focus groups and questionnaires don't cut it; designers know that you must care enough to actually be present in people's lives."*

Berger's second step urges you to care enough about the problems your users face to get out of your cube or office and meet them face-to-face. And this is more than a matter of commitment. Unless you're physically present, you can't pick up the non-verbal clues to meaning that are so essential to Design Thinking. You can't see that people are pretty frustrated with their flip-phones and Blackberrys and that some other kind of interface might help them.

> *"Connect. Designers know that you must 'think laterally' – searching far and wide for ideas and influences – and must also be willing to try*

connecting ideas that might not seem to go together. This is a way of thinking that can also be embraced by non-designers."

Berger says that connecting ideas is a shortcut to innovation. You can meet users' needs without inventing a solution from scratch. Here again, the iPhone is a model of connection. The email, telephony and other services it embodied were not new, but they were *connected* in a new way.

"Commit. It's one thing to dream up original ideas. But designers quickly take those ideas beyond the realm of imagination by giving form to them. Whether it's a napkin sketch, a prototype carved from foam rubber, or a digital mock-up, the quick-and-rough models that designers constantly create are a critical component of innovation – because when you give form to an idea, you begin to make it real."

Committing early raises the specter of failure, because early designs have rough edges. They may even head off in the wrong direction. But Berger notes that committed designers cultivate a tolerance for failure, because they know that failure is on the path to success. They're committed to fully meeting the needs that they uncover in the course of their empathetic inquiry.

Lawyers, of course, are trained *never* to fail, which means that you may need a deeper level of commitment to endure the skepticism lawyers bring to napkin sketches and other rough ideas. So commit with a vengeance!

OMG

If you're a normal BI professional, by this point in the chapter, you should be thinking "OMG, what have I gotten myself into? Let's just screw in the damn light bulb, OK?" But stay with Design Thinking a little longer to see where it might lead.

We see from Berger that the fundamental thrust of Design Thinking concerns getting to the smart question, the really telling question. And the most telling question might appear at first to be a dumb question. But you can't get deeply into somebody's life without dropping assumptions and presumptions and just asking about what you don't know. And these most fundamental questions aren't dumb, because at the foundational levels of someone else's work, you *can't* know without abandoning your ego and asking very, very basic things.

Beginning with the prosaic

OK, so we've gotten a rough feel for the "telling question" approach of Design Thinking. How does it work in practice? We could throw you off into the deep end, right at an inquiry that goes to the heart of law practice. But let's start with something simpler first. We'll begin with the truly prosaic – a business measure likely to be found inside many law firms – and work some Design Thinking on it to see what happens. As we do this, we'll be shortcutting a good deal. We can't trace all the question taxonomies that are necessary to elicit these results. Moreover, Design Thinking goes far beyond merely asking questions of interviewees, and includes the close observation of subjects to capture important verbal and nonverbal clues to deeply held beliefs. But these questions will give you the idea how Design Thinking inquiry flows and just how far you can get by starting with "dumb" questions.

Bill speed is as prosaic a measure as we're likely to find. It's the number of days it takes a lawyer, on average, to issue a bill after work is done on accounts he or she bills for. Now, there are probably a dozen different ways to handle the nuances of bill speed. But why don't we skip that? And you can throw up bill speed on your dashboards any number of ways. Should you use a speedometer dial? Because we're measuring bill *speed*! Clever, right? Or not, so maybe a bar graph? Let's skip that too.

Instead, why don't we begin looking for the telling questions about bill speed? Like, *why* do we measure bill speed? Is that a "dumb" enough question to qualify for Design Thinking? It's a starting point, anyway – an entrée into the bill speed question taxonomy.

Note that here we are directing questions towards ourselves. Doing full scale Design Thinking, we would extend the inquiries deeply into the user population and "pay no attention to the man behind the curtain." But to get a feel for the kinds of questions that flow from Design Thinking, these "thought experiments" on ourselves will do for now.

So, again, why do we measure bill speed? Is it because it's important to revenue streams? Indeed, to push the inquiry, might we do a little research or maybe even examine our own data, to find if there is a correlation between the speed with which a bill is issued and the percentage of the bill that gets paid. If you bill sooner do you get paid more? Do we measure bill speed because we want to reduce it and thereby increase revenues?

If you're good at BI, these questions are probably natural and you work through them all the time with different measures. But you can go much further using Design Thinking techniques.

For example, who is the bill speed measure meant for? Upper management, right? They're probably the one who asked for it. But is it really for them? Why, again, are we measuring bill speed?

Aren't we really trying to influence the behavior of those lawyers who prepare the draft bills, to get them to do it faster? So, we care about what's in their head, right? Design Thinking would tell us they're the real customer here, so we should be inquiring about their emotional state, their deepest feelings and beliefs. *They're* the ones we really ought to be interviewing.

We can go a long way plumbing the depths of lawyer experience. And, in the limited space of this chapter, we don't have time to work through all the possible questions we might ask, much less actually chronicle the interviews. So let's cut to the chase. Here's what you'll find if you *do* do those interviews.

After we got deeply enough into lawyer headspace, we'd find that law school was a fiercely competitive grind and that it has left a permanent mark. It both preselected candidates who are sensitive to relative positions in their cohort and it further conditioned graduates to be even more sensitive to relative rank. We would see high levels of sensitivity in connection with LSAT rankings while applying for school, in class rankings during school, and in the most certain ranking method found inside law firms after school is done – compensation. Not all lawyers are driven to maximize compensation. But a close enough study of lawyers would reveal that all are attuned to their relative rank in the firm, just as they were in law school. Once you bang around in lawyer heads long enough, you can see that relative rank evokes powerful emotions and can therefore act as a powerful force for change.

And understanding that about lawyers gives you another question to ask. In influencing lawyers to change habits like bill speed, what if we measured in relative terms, just as was done with the LSAT and in law school? What if we measured bill speed in, say, percentiles, with the fastest lawyers in the highest percentile rankings? Might that make a strong emotional connection with our users, something strong enough to influence behavior?

That's the kind of question that lets you begin an experiment – exactly the kind of experiment contemplated by Design Thinking. What you may find, if your lawyers are like the lawyers at the firm where we tried this experiment, is that relative ranking is a very direct way into the heads and hearts of lawyers. They care about it and will change behavior significantly to alter rankings. In our experiment, while absolute measures of bill speed remained essentially unchanged for years, relative ranking improved firm wide bill speed averages by more than seven days within the span of six months. And that drops money to the bottom line, both as a function of the time value of money and of increased collections percentages. Using empathy to find emotional tipping points pays.

This example is not to tout a particular way to measure bill speed. Rather, it illustrates the process by which that way of measuring was arrived at. And note that empathy doesn't always mean doing something a customer wants. Remember, no one was asking for iPhones and no lawyers were asking for relative rankings. But empathy does entail getting as deeply into the point of view of your subject as possible – *becoming* them in some sense of the word. And that skill has as much a place in BI as it does in any design discipline. Indeed, if it's not present in BI, it may be that you only wind up measuring things you can't change.

Back to the why of BI

We don't think of bill speed as a *change or die* proposition. Well, maybe – if your firm bills so slowly it's in danger of starvation. But remember, we were talking about questions that go to the heart of the delivery of legal services. What might applying Design Thinking to those most fundamental propositions look like?

Let's start with a *really* stupid question, one that's highly likely to provoke acerbic responses from the lawyers themselves, particularly if you're senior enough that they think you should know this.

What does a lawyer do?

I would contend that question is so basic that even most lawyers can't answer it, because they think they already know the answer. If you asked a lawyer "What do you do?" They might say something like "I represent high technology companies in the acquisition and protection of their assets," or "I litigate complex disputes, mainly in the financial sector."

And those answers would be right, but they're incomplete. They certainly don't go far enough to give you any hint as to what you might begin measuring to foster needed change.

So, again, what do lawyers do? If you worked your way through all the firm lawyers and back to a law department, you might get a different answer about what outside lawyers do for the companies they represent. A law department lawyer might say that outside law firms help them avoid problems and manage the problems that do occur. And by problems, mostly law departments mean lawsuits, regulatory hurdles and the like. Those are the day-to-day concerns of in-house lawyers. They might also say that outside lawyers spend their company's money.

Legal spend, you must know, is something everyone measures, inside and outside lawyers alike. But you can go much deeper than that and begin to get to real meaning.

Once you plunge deep inside a corporation, away from lawyers altogether and into the heads of those who create strategies for our corporate clients, you begin to get at what lawyers *really* do. A Peter Drucker-trained manager might say that lawyers help companies manage risk. Every day businesses continually encounter, create, trade and arbitrage risks. In some senses, risks are the real currency of business. As Drucker said:

> *"Strategic planning is the continuous process of making present entrepreneurial (risk-taking) decisions systematically and with the greatest knowledge of their futurity; organizing systematically the efforts needed to carry out these decisions; and measuring the results of these decisions against the expectations through organized, systematic feedback."*

Notice how central information gathering and measurement are to the management of entrepreneurial risks. Those are BI functions and they need not stop at the boundaries of the corporation. Indeed, because lawyers help companies manage risks, it would seem imperative that law firms also measure their impact on pools of risk.

We see some firms beginning to do this when handling large litigation portfolios, mainly in the financial sector. The notion of "risk weighted exposure" is an effort to arrive at a present value risk exposure for a single suit all the way up through an entire portfolio.

That's an important undertaking in that it permits the client corporation to make large-scale decisions in the process of managing risk. Once it is quantified, risk can be leveraged, hedged or mitigated in any number of ways.

And here again, law firms who ask stupid questions can begin to aid the corporation in managing risks. Here's a stupid question you might ask: "As against a multi-billion dollar portfolio of risk weighted exposure, are there any causes of action, defenses or counterclaims that markedly increase exposure out of normal ranges?"

Experience shows that, at least in some portfolios, the answer is yes. Some defenses, for example, have out-of-scale impacts on both cost and schedule. And that bears on the type of legal advice a firm might want to offer. If fraud counterclaims or defenses have an extraordinary impact on cost, might a firm consider *not* raising every colorable fraud claim it encounters?

Apply that kind of filter across an entire portfolio and a firm might begin to reduce overall risk-weighted exposure by significant amounts. Similar approaches might work after running regression analyses against deal terms and litigations, or various regulatory undertakings. And all of this arises from the question of what lawyers do.

The simplest questions, the stupidest, if you will, are the ones that present the most opportunity. And the canvas is still largely blank, waiting for a BI artist to finally do something transformational to the relationship between lawyer and client. All you have to be willing to do is think like a designer, and ask stupid questions.

It may be that you're not in a position now to take questions all the way past the law department and to high officers inside client corporations. But you can begin applying a Design Thinking methodology even on the most prosaic measures and achieve sometimes stunning results. The key is to be willing to venture past yourself and your own cohort and delve deeply into the heads and hearts of the people you most need to understand.

The key is empathy. And it unlocks transformational change.

www.ingramcontent.com/pod-product-compliance
Ingram Content Group UK Ltd.
Pitfield, Milton Keynes, MK11 3LW, UK
UKHW021848150926
8657IPUK00005B/137

9 781783 583447